SERVING
THE KING

SERVING THE KING

Doing Ministry in Partnership with God

A.B. SIMPSON

CHRISTIAN PUBLICATIONS
CAMP HILL, PENNSYLVANIA

Christian Publications
3825 Hartzdale Drive, Camp Hill, PA 17011

Faithful, biblical publishing since 1883

ISBN: 0-87509-593-3
LOC Catalog Card Number: 95-70302
Copyright © 1995 by Christian Publications
All rights reserved
Printed in the United States of America

95 96 97 98 99   5 4 3 2 1

Serving the King
was previously published under the title
Service for the King

CONTENTS

1   *Power for Service* *1*

2   *Motives for Service* *21*

3   *Instruments of Service* *39*

4   *Personal Responsibility* *59*

5   *Partnership with God* *79*

6   *Words for Discouraged Workers* *93*

7   *Finishing Our Work* *111*

CHAPTER 1

Power for Service

That you may know . . . his incomparably great power for us who believe. (Ephesians 1:18-19)

Man is born the most impotent creature on the face of the earth. The young animal grows into its prime while the human infant is still a helpless child. Morally, a child is even weaker. His own passions are stronger than he. Every temptation bears him away, and every surrounding influence controls and molds him.

Spiritually he is weaker still, not only impotent, but dead. Slowly he learns this humbling truth, but only by many a futile effort and painful fall. This is the meaning of Abraham's falsehood, David's double crime, Job's long siege of suffering and Peter's sad denial. "Even youths grow tired and weary, and young men stumble and fall"

(Isaiah 40:30). The strongest, the most self-confident, are the most impotent of all. And true strength and safety come when at last we learn our utter insufficiency and accept the simple paradox: "When I am weak, then I am strong" (2 Corinthians 12:10).

The Revelation of God's Power

But over against man's weakness stands the revelation of God's power. This is His first manifestation; and He comes in the mighty forces and forms of Creation and Providence. So He appears to Abraham as El Shaddai, "the Almighty God." So He comes in the redemption of Israel. He crushed before a little rod the mightiest empire on earth, divided the Red Sea and the Jordan and led His people between the parted waves. He marched before them in the pillar of cloud, leveled the walls of Jericho by a trumpet blast and routed the Canaanite hosts at Beth Horon by the artillery of heaven while the planets stood still at His servant's word. He delivered His people again and again from their outnumbering and overpowering foes, holding nations as the drop of a bucket and the small dust of the balance, weighing the mountains in scales and handling them as a man would handle the little ounce weights of the druggist's counter. He took up the isles as a very little thing, carried the government of the universe on a single shoulder, and asked as He points to the traces of His power in earth and heaven and all the past history of man: "Is anything too hard for the LORD?" (Genesis 18:14).

This is the first lesson of His teaching: "Power belongeth unto God" (Psalm 62:11, KJV). And this power He puts at our service. "I am your God," He says, "All that is in Me belongs to obedient faith." There are two great potencies in the universe— God and the believer. "With God all things are possible" (Matthew 1:26). "Everything is possible for him who believes" (Mark 19:23). It is very wonderful that God should thus harness His omnipotence to a human life and put the reins in the hands of humble faith. It is wonderful that He should say to a worm: "I am the Almighty God. Take Me, possess Me, use Me. I am your God."

Power Manifested in Christ

The power of God is manifested in Christ. He is called "the power of God and the wisdom of God" (1 Corinthians 1:24). His life was a constant embodiment of divine power—power over Satan in the wilderness and on the cross, whom He left a conquered and disarmed foe, power over demoniacal possession in human souls, power over disease in every form, power over nature in storm and tempest and in the multiplied bread which fed the 5,000 on the hills of Galilee, power over death itself in the resurrection of others, and most signally of all in His own resurrection and ascension.

This is the special exhibition of His power which the apostle here emphasizes.

His incomparably great power . . . which he exerted in Christ when he raised him from the dead and seated him at his right hand in the heavenly realms, far above all rule and authority, power and dominion, and every title that can be given, not only in the present age but also in the one to come. (Ephesians 1:19-21)

Here is a power that sets all the laws of nature at defiance, sets aside all the ordinary operations and extraordinary forces of the material world and puts its feet on all power, law and dominion. It is far above all the forces of the present world, far above the mightier powers astronomy reveals, far above all heavens. Indeed, it is far above all the beings that govern their myriad worlds, far above all the rulers of the greater world of spirits even to the throne of sovereign power and universal preeminence. It has that wondrous Man ascended, and ascended in our name, as "head over everything for the church, which is his body" (1:22-23).

All this marvelous power is possessed in common with us and may be shared with the weakest of His members. The least of them can be no less or lower than His feet. Yet, "God placed all things under his feet" (1:22), and in Him we may put our feet on the neck of every foe.

Have we known "the power of his resurrection" (1:20, KJV), and in it "his incomparably great power for us who believe"(1:19)? And have we taken this Jesus as made unto us "the power of God" (1 Corinthians 1:24)? Surely of Him men will say: "In the LORD alone are righteousness and strength" (Isaiah 45:24). Surely this was what the overcoming apostle meant when he said: "I can do everything through [Christ] who gives me strength" (Philippians 4:13).

The Power of the Gospel

The gospel is the power of God to everyone who believes (Romans 1:16). This divine power, inherent in God and manifested in Christ, is offered to us in the gospel. It is not only peace, but also power. It is in itself God's mighty instrument for saving men. It has power to break man's pride, reveal man's sin, win man's confidence and change man's destiny. It has proved stronger than the philosophy of Greece, or the strength of Rome, or the pride of Judaism. It is power. The weakness of God is stronger than men. But it also brings power. It offers man the strength of God, and it confers it. It brings pardon for all the past, and for the future the power of a new, faithful and almighty friend. He who fully receives it may live a life of victory and effectiveness. Have we found its power?

The Imparting of This Power

The Holy Spirit is the great agent in imparting this power. "You will receive power when the Holy Spirit comes on you" (Acts 1:8). He is the Spirit of power. Not only does He give the newborn soul power to receive Christ and turn from sin, but He also enters the consecrated heart as a personal guest and guide. The gift of the Holy Spirit is a distinct experience from regeneration. It is one thing for me to build a house, and another to go and reside in it personally. In regeneration the Holy Spirit builds the house. In consecration He enters it as a personal guest and makes it His permanent abode, directing and using the whole being as it is offered to Him. His coming brings:

1. Power for the spirit of sonship.

"To all who received him, to those who believed in his name, he gave the right (power, KJV) to become children of God—children born not of natural descent, nor of human decision or a husband's will, but born of God" (John 1:12-13). We are children of God by second birth. But there is more than this—even power to enter into—to know and claim and enjoy our lofty sonship. There are high born heirs who do not know their birthright. And so, "because you are sons, God sent the Spirit of his Son into our hearts, the Spirit who calls out, '*Abba*, Father'" (Galatians 4:6). Then we know what is the hope of our calling and walk worthy of God as dear children.

2. Power over sin.

Therefore, there is now no condemnation for those who are in Christ Jesus, because through Christ Jesus the law of the Spirit of life set me free from the law of sin and death. For what the law was powerless to do in that it was weakened by the sinful nature, God did by sending his own Son in the likeness of sinful man to be a sin offering. And so he condemned sin in sinful man, in order that the righteous requirements of the law might be fully met in us, who do not live according to the sinful nature but according to the Spirit. (Romans 8:1-4)

This is the power that sanctifies. Holiness is not a condition wrought in us. It is simply the Holy One in us ruling, filling. It is "the spirit of life in Christ Jesus" (8:2, KJV), controlling with the power and uniformity of a law. This, and this alone, can give power over sin. This battle is too great for man. It must be the Lord's.

3. *Power for the passive virtues of Christian character.*

"Being strengthened with all power according to his glorious might so that you may have great endurance and patience, and joyfully [give] thanks to the Father" (Colossians 1:11-12). This is the victory over self, and it is the secret of power over others. The first battlefield is the heart and the home. The one who would have power to do must first receive power to endure, yea, even "with joyfulness" (KJV). There is no mightier evidence of the power of God than just such triumphs over temper and provocation, no stronger testimony and service for Jesus than the sweetness of the subdued and quiet spirit which has so learned Christ.

4. *Power for deeper Christian experiences.*

> I pray that out of his glorious riches he may strengthen you with power through his Spirit in your inner being, so that Christ may dwell in your hearts through faith. And I pray that you, being rooted and established in love, may have power, together with all the saints, to grasp how wide and long and high and deep is the love of Christ, and to know this love that surpasses knowledge— that you may be filled to the measure of all the fullness of God. (Ephesians 3:16-19)

These words describe the highest possibilities of Christian life, and experience "immeasurably more than all we ask or imagine" (3:20). But this we cannot enter until we are first "strengthen[ed] . . . with power through his Spirit in [our] inner being" (3:16). We could not bear such a blessing in our natural strength. We don't have capacity to receive it. Our being must be enlarged; our spirit must be raised to a mightier level. Our understanding must grasp more clearly, and our faith appropriate more firmly the things that are freely given to us of God. Thus we need power to take more power. And just as the sea wave that washes in and fills the little basin on the beach, washes a larger, deeper basin by its force, and leaves larger room for the next wave, so the Holy Spirit enlarges our heart to receive still more of Himself.

5. *Power to resist temptation.*

> Be strong in the Lord and in his mighty power. . . . For our struggle is not against flesh and blood, but against the rulers, against the authorities, against the powers of this dark world and against the spiritual forces of evil in the heavenly realms. Therefore put on the full armor of God, so that when the day of evil comes, you may be able to stand your ground. (6:10-13)

How large a place temptation has in every Christian life! And the nearer we get to God the more severely it presses us. The rulers and powers of evil are "in the heavenly realms." And we have no power to resist them. We must have His power or fall. In fact we must have Himself for our power and our Overcomer or we will be overcome. "When the enemy shall come in like a flood, the Spirit of the LORD shall lift up a standard against him" (Isaiah 59:19, KJV).

Happy are they who have learned the secret of strength and victory. In all these things they are more than conquerors through Him that loved them. Hence few know much of what temptation or victory means until they have the life of power.

6. *Power for aggressive conflict against Satan.*

"I have given you authority to trample on snakes and scorpions and to overcome all the power of the enemy; nothing will harm you" (Luke 10:19). This was Christ's commission to the

70. And it is His message to every true worker in the great harvest field. He sends them forth saying, "Ask the Lord of the harvest, therefore, to send out workers into his harvest field" (Matthew 9:38).

Therefore this prayer is for all true servants. It is power over all the power of the enemy. This is not for our defense against temptation merely. This is aggressive war. This is power to cast out demons and destroy the works of the devil.

Thus the Holy Spirit came to the apostles. Filled with the Holy Spirit, Paul said to Elymas, "You are a child of the devil and an enemy of everything that is right! You are full of all kinds of deceit and trickery. Will you never stop perverting the right ways of the Lord?" (Acts 13:10). And God's judgment fell upon him. In that way also Paul flung from his hand the viper. Thus he triumphed over all the power of the enemy. He cried as he pressed on: "The Lord will rescue me from every evil attack and will bring me safely to his heavenly kingdom" (2 Timothy 4:18).

We need this power in the conflict still, and we may have it. Pastor Blumhardt prayed all night long by the side of a wild demoniac, and before the dawning light had broken, the victim arose, shouting, "Jesus is Victor!" and went forth to a life of blessed liberty and service.

7. *Power for service and testimony.*

You will receive power when the Holy Spirit comes on you; and you will be my witnesses. (Acts 1:8)

You are witnesses of these things. I am going to send you what my Father has promised; but stay in the city until you have been clothed with power from on high. (Luke 24:48-49)

Our gospel came to you not simply with words, but also with power, with the Holy Spirit and with deep conviction. (1 Thessalonians 1:5)

My message and my preaching were not with wise and persuasive words, but with a demonstration of the Spirit's power, so that your faith might not rest on men's wisdom, but on God's power. (1 Corinthians 2:4-5)

If anyone speaks, he should do it as one speaking the very words of God. If anyone serves, he should do it with the strength God provides, so that in all things God may be praised through Jesus Christ. To him be the glory and the power for ever and ever. Amen. (1 Peter 4:11)

The Apostle Paul devotes a whole chapter, First Corinthians 12, especially to explain and illustrate the gifts of the Holy Spirit for service. He begins by declaring our absolute dependence upon the

Holy Spirit even for power to bear the simplest testimony to Jesus Christ. He then shows the diversity of the Spirit's gifts, but declares that to everyone some manifestation of this divine power is given for improvement and service. He then specifies the various gifts of knowledge, wisdom, faith, miracles, healing, prophecy, tongues, discerning of spirits. Next he clearly intimates that they may all be expected in the Church of Christ through the whole Christian age. These charismata, or spiritual gifts, were clearly recognized in the early church and were designed to be zealously sought, cherished and cultivated. Service for Christ was understood not as the exercise of our natural powers and talents, but the use of the special gifts of the Great Paraclete.

The wisdom of nature was regarded as foolishness with God, and Christ was received as wisdom and utterance. The talents and the pounds were not natural endowments, but spiritual endowments. Our good works were declared to be "prepared in advance for us to do" (Ephesians 2:10), so that the weakest and humblest saint could minister "according to the grace given us" (Romans 12:6), and "with the strength God provides" (1 Peter 4:11).

Indolence, timidity and unfruitfulness were left without excuse. In themselves all were equally insufficient even to think anything as of themselves. All had equal claims to His all-sufficiency, and equal right to say: "I can do everything through him who gives me strength" (Philippians 4:13).

This power reached out alike in every direction of Christian life and service. It was as necessary for a deacon in administering the finances of a church, of a private member in giving his means to God, as to an apostle to his ministry or a saint on his knees. Every service for the Lord must be in the Holy Spirit and in the strength of Jesus, or it will not be acceptable to God. He alone is acceptable to the Father, and only His life and work in us can be accepted above. All our service, therefore, is simply partnership with Christ. It is Christ working His work in us. This was His promise when He went away. "Anyone who has faith in me will do what I have been doing. He will do even greater things than these, because I am going to the Father" (John 14:12).

That does not mean that we will do the works that He used to do, but that we will do the works He is still to do. We will do the works that He is now carrying on in His resurrection life as our Living Head, through us, the members of His body. He is the power; we are the executioners of that power. Our works are but the complement of "all that Jesus began to do and to teach" (Acts 1:1).

This power, therefore, can never exalt the possessor into self-importance. It is not his power at all, but simply Christ in him. It differs entirely from mere human power. It is not oratorical power or personal magnetism, that subtle influence which some possess in a marked degree. It is not intellectual power or logical force, the power of persuading other minds. It is not sympathetic power, the exquisite capacity to move human sympathy, kindle feeling, excite emotion and sway human hearts at will. It is not even moral power, the power to rouse the conscience, to alarm the guilty soul, to persuade men to reformation of life and conduct. All this may be merely natural. Spiritual power is far deeper and higher. It is the power of God. It brings men to feel the presence and the fear of God. It leads men to know God, to love God, to obey God, to be like God, to receive God. It is God in man leading man to God.

Elements in the Gift of Power

Some elements in this gift of power are:

1. Knowledge.

There is power in the knowledge of the Word of God, especially the plan of salvation through the Lord Jesus Christ. The Holy Spirit carries the truth with great vividness and power to the mind and enables us so to see and reveal Jesus that the sinner cannot but accept Him.

2. Wisdom and tact.

There is power in wisdom and tact, that is, holy and divinely taught discrimination and fitness of appeal, counsel and exhortation. This is knowing "the word that sustains the weary," which He "wakens [our] ear to listen like one being taught" (Isaiah 50:4). This is the power to know and speak the Lord's own message, one sentence of which is worth a volume of our well-meaning opinions and ideas.

3. Faith.

Faith is indispensable to all power. "We also believe and therefore speak" (2 Corinthians 4:13), must be true of every man who would speak with the power of God. We must have the same faith for our message and our work as for our own souls. The men of power in apostolic times were the men of faith. "Full of faith and power" (Acts 6:8, KJV), "full of faith and of the Holy Spirit" (6:5), are their brief biographies. This is no common faith. The faith of effectual service is the very faith of God and God's own omnipotence.

4. Love.

This includes all love's accompaniments—fervor of spirit, compassion, tenderness, sympathy, concern for souls, affectionateness of manner, intense longing for the salvation of men, travail of spirit for the unsaved and that deep heart power which is the greatest of all spiritual forces. Many persons lack this essential element of power. Great courage, wisdom, earnestness and force are neutralized by hardness or lack of love. Arctic explorers kindle fires from the sun by ice lenses, but he who would kindle hearts from above must be himself on fire. Your heart must overflow if you intend to reach another's heart. The Holy Spirit brings to us this element of power, even Christ's own love to men.

5. Earnestness.

Earnestness includes the intense concentration of all one's power to the work of saving men. It is a soul duly alive to its great business, to men's interests and perils, and using all its powers and energies to do them good. There is no power without earnestness so deep and strong as to raise even enthusiasm. The very word means God in a man, and the power of God in us will kindle all our powers to a flame.

6. Unction.

Unction is finer and diviner still. It is that inexpressible yet unmistakable influence which so melts and mellows our whole being. It baptizes thought, feeling, word, expression and even our very tones, looks and gestures with the Spirit of God and with His life, love and power, so that men are irresistibly impressed, subdued, attracted and convicted. We may be so pervaded by God that He can constantly show forth in us "the aroma of Christ" (2 Corinthians 2:15), that "spreads everywhere the fragrance of the knowledge of him" (2:14).

7. Conviction.

There is yet another element of power. This is the power to lead men to conviction and decision, the power to reach their conscience with the sense of God, to awaken their fear of God and consciousness of sin and to lead them to act, to decide, to choose, to be definite, immediate and thoroughly committed to the one urgent, all-important step of receiving the Savior. This power we see in Peter's sermon on the day of Pentecost, in Paul's message to the Philippian Jailer, and in the specially useful evangelists of all later times. It is indispensable for all true Christian workers. He who neglects to receive and use it will often have cause to say of the fruits of his work: "While your servant was busy here and there, the man disappeared" (1 Kings 20:40).

The Secret of Power

What is the secret of power? How can we obtain the gift of power?

1. Conscious weakness.

"He . . . increases the power of the weak" (Isaiah 40:29). We must utterly know and realize our insufficiency. We must come to the end of all our resources, power, love, thought, even faith itself. Then He comes and lives in us, our All in all.

2. Consecration.

Give your weakness to Christ to use for Himself. Dedicate to Him your power to be filled and used. Lay on His altar the gift He is about to bestow. Take it as a sacred and unselfish trust to be employed for His work and glory. And He will give abundantly. He will take the offered vessel and use it. He will feel the consecrated hand, and of His own you will serve and glorify Him.

3. Appropriating and acting faith.

Take hold of His strength. Attach your little wheel to His great engine, and it will run with heavenly power. God gives to each of us a house with power. He puts within our reach the great engine of His omnipotence and bids us attach our wheel of need for strength or service, and to take the power that is running to waste freely at our disposal.

During the Philadelphia exposition one of the most extraordinary objects in the great hall was the Corliss engine, a steam engine with sufficient power to drive all the machinery which the building could hold. All over the huge building were scattered almost all possible apparatus of industrial machinery. Not one of them had any self-moving power, but all that was necessary to put every wheel in swift and powerful motion was to attach it to the great engine. Then the little knitting machine went as freely as the great printing press, each taking from the same source of power all it could contain and use.

Even so in God's great work of life, some of us are little knitting and sewing machines and some great presses, but none of us have any power of our own. But in our midst is that Great Engine— the Holy Spirit—and we have only to attach the connecting band of faith. Then the power passes into each life according to our need and in proportion to our use of it. The humble seamstress at her sewing machine receives it as abundantly as she can take it in, as well as the author who sends his great thoughts to the world through the printing press, or the voice that speaks the messages of truth and life to listening thousands. The power meets us, helps us, carries us wherever we are and whatever our service if it be but His will. And all we need is to make the connection and then to use the power for Him. So may He enable us to take hold of His strength and give it back to Him.

CHAPTER 2

Motives for Service

Bind the sacrifice with cords, even unto the horns of the altar. (Psalm 118:27, KJV)

The sacrifice is our consecrated service to God and the cords which bind it to the altar are the motives, the impulses which ought to constrain us to a more earnest and entire devotion to Christ and to His work. God wants us so to yield ourselves, living sacrifices by the mercies of God, that we will feel bound by a thousand cords on His altar. They should be loving bonds, silken cords, that we would not break if we could.

The Bond of Redemption

The first motive which ought to hold us to serve the Lord Jesus Christ is the very fact of our redemption. We are distinctly taught that we were not redeemed in any sense at all for our own selfish advantage. "You are not your own; you were bought at a price" the apostle says very solemnly in his letter to the Corinthians. "Therefore honor God with your body" (1 Corinthians 6:19-20).

If you were to buy a house, you would think it strange if the seller should retain it for his own use and want to live in it himself and collect the rent. If you were to buy an article of value, you would be surprised if the seller should refuse to let you use it. And so the Lord has bought you—He has bought you to use you, bought you to be an instrument for His service. Even though you have not performed the consecrating act, you are bound to belong to the Lord. You were consecrated by your redemption, and you are not your own, for you were bought with a price. Consecration is just coming up to your true obligations and returning that which is simply right. The mere fact that you have been redeemed by Christ should constrain you and bind you as a cord to the altar of service.

The Bond of Salvation

Our salvation binds us to the service of Christ. We were not saved for ourselves, but in order to serve the Lord. We find this in a great many passages. Especially you will remember what Paul says about his own salvation: "But for that very reason I was shown mercy so that in me, the worst of sinners, Christ Jesus might display his unlimited patience as an example for those who would believe on him and receive eternal life" (1 Timothy 1:16).

So Paul says he was saved not for the sake of his own soul merely, but saved that he might save other souls. The very reason of his rescue from his sinful life was that he might save men in coming days. And so, if you have been saved strangely and wondrously, it is for you to save others through God as strangely and won-drously. If you have been saved from any evil, it is for you to save others from that evil. If you have been saved from some special form of sin, it is your ministry to rescue others from the same, so that your very salvation is a cord that binds you to the altar of God.

The Bond of Our Calling

Our calling and election are for service. I do not use the term here with reference to our salvation. I believe that these words, "calling and election," are used in the Scripture very emphatically with respect to our service and to our special standing as Christians after we have been saved.

When Peter says, "make your calling and elec-tion sure" (2 Peter 1:10), I do not think he means our salvation at all. Peter was referring to some higher calling that comes after our salvation—our calling to a place of service and honor, our election to an office, to a position of trust and honor. In the state men are called to positions of trust and are elected to positions of honor, and so I think God uses this word to denote our being summoned by His word and set apart by His gracious will to some place of special usefulness.

Now, we are told distinctly that we are called that we might serve. "You did not choose me," Christ said to His apostles, "but I chose you" (John 15:16). What for? That you should go to heaven? No, that you should go and bring forth fruit, that your fruit should remain, and that your prayer should be so effectual that "the Father will give you whatever you ask in my name" (15:16). That is your calling, chosen and ordained, that you should bring forth fruit and be a minister of blessing to others.

Paul summed up his calling in his testimony to King Agrippa. He related the words Christ spoke to him on the Damascus road:

> "I have appeared to you to appoint you as a servant and as a witness of what you have seen of me and what I will show you. I will rescue you from your own people and from the Gentiles. I am sending you to them to open their eyes and turn them from darkness to light, and from the power of Satan to God, so that they may receive forgiveness of sins and a place among those who are sanctified by faith in me."
>
> So then, King Agrippa, I was not disobedient to the vision from heaven. (Acts 26:16-19)

That was Paul's calling. God appeared to him in that moment to save him and give him a higher calling.

And so to you there comes a calling in life

somewhere and sometime as surely as it came to Abram in that day in Ur of Chaldea, and he went forth not knowing whither; as surely as it came to Jacob, in the vision at Bethel by night; as surely as it came to Paul on the way to Damascus. God has called you and called me to some special mission in life. It is a work that nobody else can do, and that if you do not do, you will stand at His judgment door recreant and condemned for neglect of your vocations. I don't know what your calling is. I think I know something of what mine was. And I am sure that if I had not listened and by His grace stood amid testings which made the blood quiver, I would have missed the blessings of my life, and perhaps others would have lost theirs.

God calls every one of you to some special duty. That mission for Him is the very meaning of life. Without it life would be a miserable mistake and prove a fraud at last and all the wishes and desires you spent on yourselves would be lost, and you would have lost even the thing you lived for—yourself.

The Bond of Sanctification

We are sanctified to serve God. Our sanctification is one of the cords which binds us to the altar of service. We are taught again, in another place: "How much more, then, will the blood of Christ . . . cleanse our consciences from acts that lead to death, so that we may serve the living God" (Hebrews 9:14).

I used to think that we were sanctified at last in order to go to heaven—that the very last thing God did for the soul was to sanctify it, and that then He took it right home. And I will confess that I was a good deal afraid of being sanctified, for fear I would die soon afterward. And I am also afraid many people have the idea that sanctified people are not good for anything.

But the Lord Jesus Christ tells us that we are sanctified in order to serve Him here. You cannot go forth and fight the enemy successfully until the victory is won in the citadel of your heart, in your own soul. While there is a revolution going on at home, you cannot have much foreign aggression. While sin is mastering you, you cannot do any good work for Jesus. God wants you to get your victory from sin, in order that you may live a useful life and go forth with the prestige of that victory and overcome the world and the devil. And so this blessed experience that God has brought to you for the purpose of cleansing your soul from sin means a life of service. You will not be able to keep it up if it is going to make you join a sort of holy elite circle, enjoying your own blessing, wrapped up in your own comfort. No, only as you use it to bring in others can you keep what you have. Joshua and the tribes of Israel entered into the land that they might lead their brethren into the rest. There was to be no rest for them "until the LORD gives [their brothers] rest, . . . and until they too have taken possession of the land that the LORD your God is giving them" (Joshua 1:15).

The Bond of the Holy Spirit

Another cord that binds us to the altar is the enduement of the Holy Spirit, which is given us only for service, and which we can keep only while we consecrate it to the work of Jesus. "You will receive power when the Holy Spirit comes on you; and you will be my witnesses" (Acts 1:8). That is what you receive the power for. The fact that you have received that divine Spirit is a solemn incentive and a strong motive that should lead you to use that trust for the highest ends for which God has given it. Don't waste a treasure so unspeakably valuable. Don't let it be idly wasted away and expended in mere talk, mere personal enjoyment, mere idealism. Go forward with that higher power to work for others and for God. In this way you will keep the blessing which He has given only for service and only to them that obey.

I think it was Theodore Monod who spoke about a steam engine, saying: "Suppose I go to a locomotive, and say: 'What are you good for?' 'Well, I have got power.' 'What is your power good for?' 'Well, I can make a tremendous whistle.' 'Well,' he says, 'what is the good of a whistle? I want something that can do something—that can move these cars and carry these tons of freight along the track.' "

And so, what is the good of your power if all it does is to make a whistle, proclaiming how much power you have? What God wants is the power that will carry other hearts and will bear the burdens of the Lord. How much are you bearing? What is your carrying power? That is the design of power. It is not what you say as much as what you do and bear for Jesus Christ and His cause.

This enduement of power which the Lord has given us has been given for service. God has dropped celestial fire in your breast. See to it that you kindle other fires and cover the whole world and the whole circle of your life with flames. I should be afraid—terribly afraid—to have been where many of you have been, and then relapse into an easy, self-indulgent life. I should be terribly afraid to have touched the coal of fire, as some of you have touched it, and to have bowed at His feet in solemn consecration, and today to be doing nothing for His kingdom, or doing less than God calls you to. May the Lord bind you to His altar with the cords of His own mighty indwelling and make you feel that to have God within you is a blessed privilege and a most sacred trust.

The Bond of Our Christian Experience

Again, our Christian experience is a motive to service. I mean by this that our Christian experience is given us not for our sake, but for the sakes of others. The way God leads you is intended to aid somebody else. The conflicts and victories that you have had are designed to enable you to help some fellow soldier in the strife. This is one of the deeper and mysterious principles of Christian life.

"If we are distressed," Paul says, "it is for your comfort and salvation; if we are comforted, it is for your comfort, which produces in you patient endurance" (2 Corinthians 1:6). "The God of all comfort, . . . comforts us in all our troubles, so that we can comfort those in any trouble with the comfort we ourselves have received from God" (1:3-4).

The strange furnace through which you passed was just a special instruction for the instrumentality which God was making out of you. The almost martyr-like sufferings that still make you quiver and ache were to enable you to sympathize with some other suffering soul. Therefore, no matter how God leads you, don't question Him. Rather say: "Lord, what does it mean? How can I consecrate it to You? I give my trials to You. I give my experience to You. I bind my life on Your altar by these quivering heart-cords of pain or joy to be Yours alike in both."

The Bond of Our Character

Our Christian character needs service for its development and its strength. The young convert of Gadara desired, we are told, to be with Christ as soon as he was saved. But Christ would not allow him to be. He told him: "Go home to your family and tell them how much the Lord has done for you, and how he has had mercy on you" (Mark 5:19). And he went home and published through Decapolis what great things the Lord had done. A poor, weak convert, afraid to be alone, he naturally clung to Jesus' side. But the Master knew he

needed a firmer discipline, and so He said: "Go
through the cities of northeastern Galilee, and tell
them what you were and what you are. Get yourself so committed that you cannot go back again.
And every word you speak and every testimony
you give will grow stronger and bolder and more
committed to Me, until you so become My repre-
sentative that you could not turn recreant to Me
even if you attempted to." And so this poor fellow,
fresh from Christ, went as a missionary through
that Eastern land. Before three months had passed
the whole region on that side of Galilee was wonderfully awakened, and they gathered together in
such multitudes that Jesus had to feed the 4,000
on the shores of the lake and could not send them
away. But this poor fellow was the strongest of
them all, and out of all the good he did, the best
was the good he got. A young disciple, to grow
strong must testify to what God has given to him.
He must stand up for Christ fearlessly, uncompro-
misingly, and his Christian life must bind him as a
sacrifice on the altar of the service of Jesus.

Someone has drawn a beautiful figure of a little
mountain stream starting down from the hills. It
was a little tiny thing, not more than a foot wide
and two or three inches deep, skipping over the
rocks and dancing along the cataracts, flowing
through the meadows and bearing away down to
the sea. As it went along it passed a great big pool
of water. The pool spoke up and said: "Why so
fast? Why are you in such a hurry? Why don't
you be quiet like me? You seem to be very free

with your water. You seem to forget that summer is coming on and you will be very glad to have a little of that abundance then that you are throwing away now so recklessly dashing around you. You must be forgetting the hot days that are coming. Why don't you keep your treasures as I do?" But the little stream only answered by the dash of its waters over the rocks and went on, not stopping to answer, pouring its water generously away. And so the spring and the summer came. It was not long until the pool began to find itself deserted. The very cattle of the wilderness were afraid to come near it. The birds would not rest in the branches above it. A filthy smell arose from its stagnant waters. The air caught the malaria and bore it along through the plains. But the little dancing river went dancing on. And the branches of the trees spread themselves over, and the cattle came to drink, and the little birds sat by its banks and the more it ran, the deeper it grew—a great river supplying the people with water and pouring its overflow into the great sea.

Don't be like the stagnant pool. Don't be like the Christian who keeps what he has hermetically sealed in his heart and pocketbook. Be like the little stream growing as it gives, for the more we give the more we get. "What I kept, that I lost. What I gave, that I have," is the epitaph on an old tombstone, which we might well remember. And so, dear friend, if you would have the richest Christian character, if you would have the full tide of heavenly power, be like the little stream—give, and in giving you will grow.

You might think as you look at your bathtub in your house full of water that there was a great deal more water there than in the little lead pipe that connects it. That little inch pipe you would think could not hold as much water as the basin. But I tell you that in the course of 24 hours there is 10 times more water that goes through that little inch pipe than is contained in the larger basin. Why? Because it is a conduit pipe. It is giving as it receives. I would rather be a little conduit pipe than the reservoir, which seems the larger, but is not really so. For your own Christian character and life as well as for the Lord, give yourself to a useful consecrated life.

The Bond of Our Happiness

Then, our happiness, our real joy, ought to bind us to the altar of service. I mean by that that a life of usefulness is the only happy Christian life. Blessed are the pure in heart. Blessed is the man whose sin is forgiven. Blessed are those who hunger, etc. There are a score of "blesseds"! There is one "more blessed," but it is better than them all. "It is more blessed to give than to receive" (Acts 20:35). It is one of the speeches of Jesus which Matthew, Mark, Luke and John have omitted. It is one of the little words of Christ that is not recorded there, but God thought so much of it that He made it a little fifth gospel. Paul caught it up before it was lost and has given it to us. And I am so glad he did, for in some respects it transcends any of the others. It makes you glad; it saves you from a thousand petty self-seeming cares and trials.

Someone has said in poetry:

Wouldst thou from sorrow find a sweet
relief,
Or wouldst thou seek support for woes
untold,
Balm wouldst thou gather for corroding
grief,
Pour blessings round thee like a shower of
gold?
'Tis when the rose is wrapped in many a
fold,
Close to its heart the worm is wasting there.

Many are living in a little world of their own trouble and sorrow. I never knew a sad soul yet that had broken out from life thus to go and live for Christ and for others. It is not possible to be overcome by grief and depression when you rise into the life of love. It is yourself that makes you morose because you are losing something or suffering something. It is the curse of Satan. It was the thing that made the devil a devil. He ceased to live for God and began to live for himself. It will make anybody a devil, unless he turns from it. Self-love, self-pride, self-care, how they cling to you with such an instinct of fear that you are going to lose something. How sad it is! It is the cause of all your miseries. But if you would live for others and be large-hearted and consecrated, if you would be happy, if your cares would be exchanged for His, then you would cease to bear your burdens and you would bear your Master's. And remember, He says that His yoke is easy and His burden is light (Matthew 11:30).

But there is a deeper joy. There is the joy of Christ's love and Christ's benevolence and sympathy for others. Do you know what it is? Some of you do. There is no deeper joy in Christian hearts, perhaps, than the joy of bringing souls to Christ, the joy of seeing lives transformed, wrecked homes made happy and souls forever saved. This is the joy that comes from the service of God. May it bind your hearts and lives on the altar of God, a living sacrifice.

The Bond of the Human Soul

Another of the cords that ought to bind us is the value of the soul—the preciousness of the human soul. It seems there can be no motive stronger than this. Paul was bound upon the altar by this cord. "I have great sorrow and unceasing anguish in my heart," he said, "for the sake of my brothers" (Romans 9:2-3)—those that were not saved. Those that have looked into eternity and have measured the value of Christ's blood and Christ's warnings and invitations feel likewise that they cannot rest while there will be one soul unsaved that they can rescue. As Richard Knill used to say:

"If there were but one man alive on earth unsaved and that one man was in Siberia, and it was necessary that to save him every

Christian in the world should go to him and plead with him, it would be worthwhile for all the fifteen hundred million people on the earth to go and plead with that one man. For eternity is so immeasurably long, and misery and joy forever mean so much, that it would repay us."

We do not see it now, dear friend, but we just have flashes of it. But when the lurid clouds of the great day will be around us and the vanities of earth will be drifting like smoke and lost men like chaff in the storm, those that you have known will look back with one upbraiding glance. And the Lord will look on you as if to say: "Was this all you cared for Me?" We will understand it then! May God help us to know it better, to preach as if we saw it, to pray as if we felt it and to labor for it as for our own salvation.

The Bond of Our Service Opportunities

Our opportunities for service give another powerful incentive to work for Christ. Every such opportunity is a direct call of God. The special openings for service which we find in this day on every hand seem to say to us as never before: "Who knows but that you have come to royal position for such a time as this?" (Esther 4:14).

There never was a time when deeper tides were moving in human hearts and a profounder hunger was crying for a living God and a full salvation. A silent revolution is passing over the Church of God in which men and women are awaking to the need of something greater than ideas, organizations and works, and must have life and power. It is a time for earnest work and testimony. May God give us understanding of the times to know what we ought to do (1 Chronicles 12:3), and make us prompt and wise and true. It is harvest time and harvest work does not wait for our convenience. It is urgent work, immediate work, work which cries: "Son, go and work today in the vineyard" (Matthew 21:28). By every call of opportunity "bind the sacrifice with cords, even unto the horns of the altar" (Psalm 118:27, KJV).

The Bond of Christ's Resources

Another bond of obligation is found in the ample resources which Christ has given us for His work. If He sent us in our own strength or inadequately furnished, we might, perhaps, plead some excuse. But He has provided all grace so that we "in all things at all times, having all that [we] need, [we] will abound in every good work" (2 Corinthians 9:8).

The talents in the parable of Matthew 25 and the pounds in that of Luke 19 do not denote our natural endowments of mind or circumstances. They are those free gifts of the Holy Spirit which are "given for the common good" (1 Corinthians 12:7). We have but to take freely of His abundant grace and use it for His work. This renders the plea of weakness inexcusable and makes the sin of neglecting such costly divine provision very great indeed. Let us "therefore, since we are receiving a kingdom that cannot be shaken, let us be thankful, and so worship (serve, KJV) God acceptably with reverence and awe" (Hebrews 12:28).

The Bond of Our Reward

Another bond and impulse of service is the great reward which He has promised to those who faithfully follow Him in the path of labor and suffering. They "will shine like the brightness of the heavens, . . . like the stars for ever and ever" (Daniel 12:3). "To him who overcomes, I will give the right to sit with me on my throne" (Revelation 3:21). When we see that reward we will be ashamed of our hardest sacrifice. Then we will cry: "Not to us, O LORD, not to us but to your name be the glory" (Psalm 115:1). Ten cities for 10 pounds well spent, an exceeding and eternal weight of glory for every weight of toil and pain. It will seem too much for such poor work, and we will cast the crowns at His blessed feet and cry: "You alone are worthy to receive glory."

The Bond of His Love

Finally, His own dear love to each one of us is the strongest cord. Think how He has saved us, loved us, led us and blessed us. The highest offering is "little to give to Him," as a dying mother said when asked if she could give up her darling children.

"Do you always feel thus?" they asked the pilgrim. "When I look at my white garments, which the shining ones gave me, that will do it; and when I look at yonder celestial hills and think of the City, whither I am going, that will do it; and when I look back to the cross where He died for me and where I lost my burden, that will do it." So let us look in and look back and look forward, and "bind the sacrifice with cords, even unto the horns of the altar" (Psalm 118:27).

CHAPTER 3

Instruments of Service

But God chose the foolish things of the world to shame the wise; God chose the weak things of the world to shame the strong. He chose the lowly things of this world and the despised things—and the things that are not—to nullify the things that are, so that no one may boast before him. It is because of him that you are in Christ Jesus, who has become for us wisdom from God—that is, our righteousness, holiness and redemption. Therefore, as it is written: "Let him who boasts boast in the Lord." (1 Corinthians 1:27-31)

This passage gives us an inventory of God's favorite instruments—of the things that God likes best to use, and the people that God especially chooses. And some of you may be surprised to find yourselves not included in this inventory.

Some of you may feel that it would be a considerable humiliation to come within it. You have your choice of five places: you can either be among the foolish things, or among the weak things, or among the lowly things, or among the despised things, or among the things that are not at all. It is in one or the other of these classes you will have to muster if you are going to be one of God's favorite instruments and one of the things which God has chosen to amount to anything to nullify the things that are strong and wrong.

The Foolish Things

The Corinthians were terribly chagrined at the humiliation of having to give up their culture. It was a sort of modern Boston or Edinburgh—very proud of its culture. And so when Apollos came among them and began to preach the philosophy of the Alexandrian school of which he was master, they were delighted with him. They turned away from the crude and barren style of old Paul and thought they had found something worthy to be compared with their wisdom. But Paul told them that God holds all this culture in great derision, that He thinks very little of it. Indeed, that it is foolishness with Him. And that if any man will be wise, he must become a fool that he may be wise. That is, he must abandon his own natural and self-confident wisdom. He must be willing to esteem as of very little value the product of his own intellect and his education, and like a little child begin at the alphabet at the feet of Jesus. "For the wisdom of this world is foolishness in God's sight. As it is written: 'He catches the wise in their craftiness' " (1 Corinthians 3:19).

There is a great deal of danger in our modern American life of this same thing. There is an affectation of culture, and perhaps a real culture, which is beginning to become a kind of god to the higher classes of American society. Enormous sums are spent on a few special works of art in this city—hundreds of thousands of dollars at a single sale, enough to sustain the gospel for half a century in the great mission fields. People ought to pause a little and remember that natural culture has often been associated with the world's darkest ages. The man who built the first city, made the first musical instrument, and constructed the first works of human industry and art was Cain. And since that day the world, when it goes away from God, tries to make the earth a paradise.

The next great land of culture was Egypt, but God took His people right out of Egypt and He did not preserve among them one single trace of Egyptian science, Egyptian art, Egyptian culture. He would not let them touch a work of art, lest it should be made subservient to idolatry. The next great period of culture was perhaps in Babylon, the cradle of Grecian culture. But what did that come to? "Is not this the great Babylon I have built . . . by my mighty power and for the glory of my majesty?" In that same hour there came a voice from heaven: "Your royal authority has been taken from you. You . . . will live with the wild animals" (Daniel 4:30-33). Then Nebuchadnezzar went out under the strongest form of madness until he learned that every man's pride must be laid low at the feet of God.

The next stage of culture we find in Greece, perhaps the highest stage that has ever been attained in the history of man. And what was Grecian culture and art when Paul looked upon its most splendid monuments in Athens? You do not find a bit of enthusiasm such as modern travelers display, but his spirit was stirred within him when he saw the city given to idolatry. Every particle of it was a minister of idolatry; every particle of it was the handmaid of sin. And it did not save Greece from the deepest moral degradation.

The next and the most brilliant period of art and culture the world had ever seen was the modern Italian age when Raphael and Michelangelo gave the world their triumphs of genius. You will remember that was the time when Caesar Borgia sat in the Papal chair, a monster of infamous iniquity. It was a time when the church was sunk in utter corruption, though its temples were adorned with the most splendid paintings.

Now, I do not say that culture is necessarily wrong. I do not say that intellect and education may not go hand in hand with Christianity. I do not deny that the Reformation brought a revival of true literature. But I do say that to pursue culture for its own sake estranges one from God. To follow the sole guidance of the human mind and to depend upon it instead of God's holy Word and

God's higher will as the basis of character and life, is always fatal, both to morality and to religion. And I believe that today we are just hastening to that point when Daniel's vision will come true: "Many will go here and there to increase knowledge. . . . but the wicked will continue to be wicked" (Daniel 12:4, 10), and then the Lord will come. This is to be the last picture of the days before Christ's return. It is a picture of human smartness such as has never been known before, and human infamy, such as has never been dreamed of before.

Paul therefore tells these Greeks that their wisdom, knowledge, skill, intelligence and philosophy will not make men wise. "Although they claimed to be wise, they became fools and exchanged the glory of the immortal God for images made to look like mortal man . . . and worshiped and served created things rather than the Creator" (Romans 1:22-25).

God is not going to save the world by brilliant intellects, or magnificent talent, but by the foolishness of preaching and the simplicity of the cross and faith in the Lord Jesus Christ. And if any man is going to be much used by God he must not depend upon his brain; he must not depend upon his social power; he must not depend upon his wealth; he must not depend upon his influence. He must put all these aside and go forth armed with the simple power of Jesus Christ's own Word and Spirit, for God has chosen the foolish things. That does not mean the silly, absurd things, but the things that have not the strength of human wisdom. God is not going to save the world today by the men of genius; God is not going to save the world today by the men of the largest talents. He is going to take average minds, and very humble minds sometimes, and very crude and very illiterate minds sometimes. Then He will enlighten them by His Holy Spirit, and give them His holy Word and glorify His own name by the very simplicity of the instruments which He employs.

Now, we see this all through God's Word. How absurd it must have seemed to the people of Jericho when an army of 600,000 men marched around their city, armed with rams' horns, and amid the blare of these instruments issued a challenge for Jericho to surrender. It was a foolish instrument, but God used that foolishness to confound all their wisdom. And before a week ended, the echo of their shout was answered by the roar and crash of falling walls and the shrieks of a city doomed to destruction.

It seemed a very foolish thing when Jesus Christ told His disciples to take a few loaves and fishes and feed a crowd of 5,000 men and perhaps 10,000 women and children. It was foolishness in the sight of man. It was an inadequate supply for such an enormous number. It was foolish in man's judgment, but God proved that the foolishness of God is wiser than man.

It seemed absurd when a few humble fishermen were sent to confront the pride and wisdom of the Jewish synagogue. But these humble fishermen and these plain men were not only able to withstand all the combined wisdom or the spirit with which they spoke. And the simple crude gospel of Christ and Him crucified had proved mightier than all the power of Greece and Rome. Before the first century had closed, the gospel had brought the wisdom of the world to the foot of the cross.

And so in these last days God has raised up from time to time this simple class of instruments—men who have been despised perhaps for their lack of culture. Since the days of the apostles there had not been such a deep and wide-spread and general awakening as God had wrought by the simple American evangelist who could not always pronounce English words correctly, and who was not afraid to acknowledge it. I am always glad to bear witness to that dear servant of God. The very highest triumphs of Dwight L. Moody's evangelistic work were in the centers of culture. There was no place in all England where the multitudes gathered with such absolutely broken and open-hearted acceptance as in the very cities of Oxford and Cambridge, in the very face of learning and scoffing pride. They had derided the idea of his coming and went to the meetings prepared to turn them into ridicule. But yet in these very places the simple, straightforward message of Jesus was greater than all their scorn. It brought hundreds and hundreds of these proud men as humble penitents to His side. The most glorious examples of missionary zeal were some of these same young men, who preached the gospel in China. God did it to show that His foolishness was stronger than man's wisdom. If you are not ashamed of your simplicity and will obey God, He can use a very small brain and a very small stock of English words and phrases and a very small amount of English grammar to glorify His name.

The Weak Things

If you don't like to take your place among the foolish things, the weak things come next in the scale of honor.

There could not be anything weaker than Moses' staff, and yet when God sent him against the mightiest empire of the past, Moses asked Him what he was to take. He said: "What is that in your hand?" and Moses said: "A staff" (Exodus 4:2). That was enough. That staff broke the throne of Pharaoh, opened the rivers and the skies in judgment, divided the sea and opened a way for God's army to pass over. It brought the dark winged angel of death over every home in Egypt, and at last shattered Pharaoh and his army on the shores of the Egyptian sea. That little rod in Moses' hand had been one of the weak things and it confounded the mighty.

There could not be anything weaker than Gideon's band of 300 men armed with a few pitchers with torches in the center, and a trumpet in the other hand. Almost as foolish as Joshua's rams' horns, these 300 men were stronger than

30,000. You remember that God had to send back the multitudes, because there were too many for Him to use. They were not weak enough for victory. When He got them so that they saw no strength but His, then power and victory came to them.

It seemed much wiser and much stronger for David to put on Saul's armor when he went against the gigantic Goliath. Saul himself tried to induce him to put on the armor, but he refused to touch them. Armed with his little sling and his five stones from the valley, he went out weak enough for victory and for God to use him. And God did use him as the type of all those victories which He promised us: " 'Not by might nor by power, but by my Spirit,' says the LORD Almighty" (Zechariah 4:6). All the armies of Saul could not even attack the Philistines. Two helpless men put them to flight because they were weak enough to depend upon God and give Him all the glory.

Even Samson, with all his physical strength, could not be used of God until God put a weak and foolish instrument into his hand, the jaw-bone of an ass, that God might be the more glorified.

And the Lord sent out His apostles—sent them out in their weakness. They were a little band without any earthly influence or power or prestige, and He told them that their very weakness was their strength. Paul says: "When I am weak, than I am strong," and "I will boast all the more gladly about my weaknesses, so that Christ's power may rest on me" (2 Corinthians 12:10, 9).

> He gives strength to the weary
>   and increases the power of the weak.
> Even youths grow tired and weary,
>   and young men stumble and fall;
> but those who hope in the LORD
>   will renew their strength.
>   (Isaiah 40:29-31)

It is a strange paradox, I know, but it certainly has been true for me, and I am certain that many others have found it true as well. The man who received the judgment of retribution was the man that had only one talent. And so, the great danger, dear friend, if you and I fail, is just the fear of our weakness. God is calling the average workers, the little ones. His army is made up of the rank and file, of such as you. And be very careful that you do not commit a sin through that very weakness, because to be unduly self-conscious of your weakness is to be just as selfish as if you were making a great deal of your strength. How often God has done through a little child what great and strong men could not do! How many a hard heart has been broken by the simple, tender words of a lisping infant, that all the wisdom of man, that all the arguments of science could not break!

A very brilliant and useful minister of the gospel, who in his early years was an ambitious politician, was elected to congress. He served several terms, got into an ambitious life and had no interest in religion. He refused all the appeals of letters and sermons and urgencies of friends and was going on in his high career of success and of near infidelity. One day, as he returned from congress, his little three-year-old girl came up to him and said, "Papa, do you know I can read?" And he said, "Darling, can you read?" And she said, "Yes." "Let me hear you," said her father, and she took up a little Testament and read: "T-h-o-u s-h-a-l-t l-o-v-e t-h-e L-o-r-d w-i-t-h a-l-l t-h-y h-e-a-r-t." She looked up in his face and tears and smiles were dancing there together. She did not understand why it was that the tears came into her father's eyes too. He took her on his lap and pressed her and kissed her over and over again. And he said, "Yes, darling, it is lovely; I am so glad you can read." He went from that nursery and on his knees before God he took the wounded heart that that little arrow pierced. He did not rest until he could say, "Yes, Lord, I, too, love You with all my heart." But that little word was the word that saved him.

A very learned minister preached a series of sermons on infidelity for the benefit of a very learned man in his church. There were some seven sermons, and he rendered them to his entire satisfaction. Soon after he got through, the infidel came to him and said that he was a Christian and had accepted the Lord Jesus Christ. The minister was very gratified. He took all the credit to himself. After it was all talked over he said, "Now, my dear friend, will you tell me which of my lectures it was that convinced you?" He said, "Sir, it was not any of your lectures. It was that poor hobbling black woman, who, when she came out, would mutter among her tears, 'My precious Savior, my precious Savior; I could not live without You!' And I watched that woman and saw that it came right straight from her heart. I did not hear all that you said, but I was deeply attracted by what she said. It was that which convinced me." It was one of the weak things of the world that God uses to confound the mighty.

Do not be ashamed to do a little for God. Remember that the vast fields of the summer are made by little blades of grass; the foliage of the forest is made by little leaves; the joys of life are made out of little tokens of love. I would rather give away all the great things in life than lose the little ones. I could not get on without them. And so God wants the humble services, the little ones. You who have just one talent, it is precious to God and it is very precious for your reward. Do not lose it, but be one of the things that God uses to confound the mighty.

The Lowly Things

This means the things that are either humble in their human relationship or associated with sin and with shame in their moral character and antecedents. God loves to take the things that men consider low and use them to confound the things that men consider high. How often has He placed men on the thrones of earth who came from the very kitchens of their masters and who were despised as menial servants. Moses was the son of a slave, and yet it was the slave's child that conquered the proud Pharaoh.

As I look back on the men and women that have told on society and on Christian life and work, I think I can say that among my fellow-students and acquaintances they have been the children of the poor. They have been the boys and girls who fought with toil and adversity and won by energy and courage the success that God has given.

Someone in giving the biography of the past two centuries said: "Some have succeeded by wealth, some by genius, some by influence, but the most of them by beginning without a penny." God "raises the poor from the dust and lifts the needy from the ash heap; he seats them with princes" (1 Samuel 2:8).

There is no rank of usefulness that God will withhold from you if you are not afraid, like the children of Joseph, to go forth and conquer the hard places. "Give us a double inheritance," they said to the Lord. "You shall have it," He said, "if you are willing to conquer it in the face of difficulties," and so God says to every one.

But among the things that God uses are also the things that were sinful. Those who are in the lowest scale of morality are the ones whom God has chosen and cleansed and made His instruments of blessing. It has been so strange to me that all through the pedigree of the Son of God it has pleased the Father to link in the most ignoble and once unworthy names. So that as we read the ancestry of Jesus we find mixed up in it in the regular line the name of Tamar, the daughter of Judah, who had the mark of deceit on her life and the name Rahab, the abandoned woman of Jericho, who believed and was chosen to be a link in the motherhood of Christ, that no one should glory in His presence. And then again, even Mary through whom He came, while pure and holy as heaven itself, yet was lowly in her social standing. And she ever bore the shame before the world of a strange misunderstanding.

Yes, the Lord has been pleased to take these things, and you know today that He has taken His Bunyans from the cursing, swearing, sinful crowds. He has taken His Jerry McAuleys from the prisons, His Morehouses from the pickpockets and His Richard Weavers from the lowest ranks of sin. He has chosen them to be His ministers that no one should glory in His presence and to prove the power of the grace of God to use the most unworthy if only surrendered to His hands.

Dear friend, has there been sin in your life? Is everything naturally against you? Have you been one of these that the Lord would be glad to choose, just to show by the very extent to which He lifts you up, the power of His infinite grace?

The Despised Things

God cannot use anybody very much without men persecuting him. "Woe to you when all men speak well of you" (Luke 6:26) is a strange and sadly true sentence of our tender Master. It was the despised Hebrews that God used to destroy the Egyptians. It was when their enemies were saying, "What are those feeble Jews doing?" (Nehemiah 4:2), that God built up the walls of Jerusalem. It was when the poor fellow was put out of the synagogue that Jesus found him and said, "Have they put you out? Well, I will take you in," and He sent him forth as the chosen instrument to put to confusion those proud men.

So it was that the Methodists in the days of Wesley got their nickname. And the people who were ridiculed, that received this very name as a nickname, today have followers in every land beneath the face of the sun. And today, when I hear men laughing, jeering and scorning, I say, "Laugh on for the Lord has another laugh, and He will always turn it on the other side. Let them curse on; the Lord will requite me blessing for their cursing this day." Do not be afraid to stand among the poor, despised company of Jesus, if it is in the name of Jesus, for the work of God and for the salvation of men. God is just going to use such things. He has chosen the despised ones to bring to nothing the proud ones.

How very often I have seen some very feeble, simple-minded one come into our work who seemed almost to be lacking in something. And I have heard good and well-meaning people say, "Now, you need not expect anything of this person." And, do you know, I have never seen yet but that God has taken hold of that person and done some wondrous thing for him. Some of the most marked cases of divine healing I have ever seen were people who were so weak that people would say, "They haven't anything in them." But the Lord said, "I will vindicate them." I remember getting almost impatient with two persons. It seemed they were so unreasonable that I could not expect anything, and I had no sooner made up my mind than God took up those people and made them the very monuments of His love and power. Then I said, "Praise the Lord!" I am afraid to think little of anybody. I am afraid to let the faintest shadow of deprecation pass my lips about the humblest and the lowest of His dear children, for I am always expecting Him to come fast behind with horses and chariots of salvation and lift them up and make them ride by His side.

There was a poor fellow who had been promoted from the ranks, and the officers were making fun of him. The colonel saw it, and he said, "Captain, I want you to come and lunch with me." After lunch was over, the colonel took his arm, and they marched up and down in front of the others' tents, arm in arm. These foolish English officers had laughed and scorned, but the next time they met him their hats were off. The colonel had taken him by his side.

When the Lord takes people to ride or walk with Him, we can safely go along. Let us be careful lest we be found despising. The Lord knows a little about scorn as well as you. "He mocks proud mockers but gives grace to the humble" (Proverbs 3:34). And He has chosen the things that are despised to confound the things that are proud. The banner of our calling is the cross of shame; and so the offense of that cross will last until He comes again. Out of the darkness and the blush of man's reproach will come the glory to our crown. And we will not be sorry at one reproach, feel not one blush of shame for which He said, "Instead of [your] shame [you] will receive a double portion!" How often has He said that to me: "For your shame you will have double"—just twice as much as if you did not have the shame— "and everlasting joy will be [yours]" (Isaiah 61:7).

The Things That Are Not

These are His last favored ones. God has chosen "the things that are not—to nullify the things that are" (1 Corinthians 1:28). That means that God cannot make anything out of you until you not only get lowly and weak, but until you get utterly dead, so that you are not at all. It is a good thing to be weak, and it is a good thing to be willing to be despised, but it is better than all to be nothing at all, to cease to be. It is better to be able to say: "I live—no, I made a mistake; not I, but Christ lives in me" (see Galatians 2:20). That is the meaning of the things that are not. God could not use Abraham until Abraham was so yielded up that even his Isaac was given over to the Lord with such simple trust that he just believed that the Lord knew all about it and would do better than he could understand. Joshua could not enter the land of Canaan until he got out of the way. It was not enough that they had crossed the Jordan. It was not enough that Moses had died. It was not enough that they had been circumcised. But then the angel met

Joshua and said: "Joshua down on your face and get out of the way." And Joshua said: "Who are you?" And He said: "I am captain." "Why, I thought I was captain," Joshua no doubt thought. "I thought you had told me to take the land." "No, I am captain," said the angel. "Take off your shoes and get down on your face." And Joshua got down on his face, and said: "What message does my Lord have for his servant?" (see Joshua 5:13-14). Joshua was dead. He was one of the things that are not, and God could use him to nullify the things that are.

Peter could not be used by the Lord until he killed himself by his denial. He had to put his pride and confidence away. He had to get down in the dust, be shamed and discouraged. Then the Lord came to him when Peter was gone, lifted him up and gave him a new commission.

Paul was not used by God until he gave up his name Saul, and took the name Paul, "the little." Paul said: "I am less than the least of all God's people" (Ephesians 3:8); "I . . . do not even deserve to be called an apostle" (1 Corinthians 15:9); "the worst of sinners" (1 Timothy 1:16). "I no longer live, but Christ lives in me" (Galatians 2:20). Then the Lord lived, the Lord reigned, and the Lord used him.

Are You Willing to Be Used?

These are the things that God uses. Are you willing to be one of them? If you are, then the blessed assurance is yours: "It is because of him that you are in Christ Jesus, who has become for us wisdom from God—that is, our righteousness, holiness and redemption. Therefore . . . 'Let him who boasts boast in the Lord' " (1 Corinthians 1:30-31).

If you are weak, if you are dead, if you are nothing, rise up now on your feet, put on the new life, put on the Lord Jesus Christ. He will be your wisdom and He will be your strength, and in His sufficiency you can do all things.

Let us not then be so occupied with the thought of what we are not, as what we are in Christ. His last thought, His last word, is the word of all-sufficiency. I know so many people who say, "I am nothing; I can do nothing." God wants you to go farther: "I am nothing; I can do all things in Him." May the Lord help us to take that place and standing today so that we will know the full meaning of these two great words: My *insufficiency*, Christ's *all-sufficiency*.

CHAPTER 4

Personal Responsibility

If anyone says anything to you, tell him that the Lord needs them. . . .

"Say to the Daughter of Zion,
 'See, your king comes to you,
 gentle and riding on a donkey,
  on a colt, the foal of a donkey.' " (Matthew 21:3, 5)

There were few in these days of our Lord who had not either seen or heard of a Roman triumphal procession, or witnessed on a smaller scale the pageants of Herod. And they had heard all over the world of the majestic and magnificent entrance to the capital of returning consuls and generals and emperors after some great victory. For days before the city was clothed in holiday attire,

59

everything was suspended but pleasure and pomp. At the appointed time the procession began to move along the sacred way toward the capital. It was preceded by great masses of splendid soldiers in perfect discipline and uniform, followed by long trains of captives, including kings and princes, and sometimes queens and beautiful women, walking in chains before the victor, while great multitudes of cattle for the sacrificial altar followed next behind. And then came the king or general himself in a gorgeous chariot drawn by many horses, clothed with every color of splendor and followed by the vast train of the people given up to the carnival and revelry, until at last the pageant reached the steps of the capitol. Then some of those queens and kings and princesses would be taken aside and executed there, as the first sacrifice of the cruel, selfish triumph. Then the cattle were slain and offered in sacrifice to their heathen gods. So the mighty Caesar or some of his satellites would show himself to be king. That was the human kingdom: that was man's stairway to a throne, and it was covered with cruelty and selfishness and blood.

The dear Lord Jesus in this chapter gives us His triumphal procession. He, too, was marching to a throne and to a kingdom. For 33 years He had been stepping up to it by the slow ascension of suffering and love. He refused from the devil the kingdoms of the world and the glory of them in a moment of time. He could take His kingdom from His father only—the pathway of blood and sorrow and holy ministering love. And then, after long refusing earthly glories, after refusing the Galileans His consent to make Him a king, after passing so long through the pathway of obscurity, at last He put aside the veil and let them see Him in His true royalty and His kingly glory. Then He began to ascend the throne which for a little while only He would keep, but by and by He will sit upon it forever.

Starting first from Jericho, He began by healing poor Bartimeus, and then saving Zacchaeus. Then He passed on to the home of Bethany\ and was anointed by Mary, and then the next morning He passed on down the slopes of Olivet. Two of His disciples were sent before Him to prepare the way. A little donkey and its colt upon which no man had ever sat were the chariots which He used—sitting upon the lowliest, most common-place of burden bearers, one that was used for toil and the meanest drudgery. On that little beast of burden He sat down, with the garments of His disciples as His trappings. Then the multitude strewed the way with palm branches, and the little children cried: "Hosanna to the Son of David!" (Matthew 21:9). The multitude joined the procession, for there were three million people at this time gathered around Jerusalem. It was the feast time. On every side hundreds of thousands of them were dwelling in little tents on the hillsides. They must have heard the sounds and flocked around and joined them, until there was as vast a procession, perhaps, as ever accompanied Caesar to his throne. And, in the midst, rode the royal Nazarene, meek and lowly, and sitting upon a donkey.

On the way, He paused just before the descent and gazed on the city. There was no light of triumph on His brow that day. There was no self-glorying in that face, as He halted and looked down on the city at His feet. He gazed a moment, and then there burst from His eyes great floods of tears, and He wept and wept again in the hour of His triumph, and said: "If you, even you, had only known . . . what would bring you peace—but now it is hidden from your eyes" (Luke 19:42). And then He passed into the temple, and as a King claimed His place as its Master, driving out the earthliness and claiming it for His Father and Himself. He stood there in the face of His enemies teaching and healing for a whole week, defying them to arrest Him until His hour had come. He was a king in every sense—of wisdom, power, suffering and love. He showed Himself there as a King.

The King

First, we see Him as the King of human hearts. He began His royal march at Bethany and received first from Mary the offering of her love. Then, next we see Him as the King of the Jews, the Son of David, claiming the throne of Jerusalem, which He is yet to restore and possess. Then we see Him as the King of the Temple, stepping into His own house and saying, "My house" (19:45). Three years before He had performed a similar miracle, and said, "My Father's house" (John 2:16). But this time He called it "My house," and He cleansed it by His word. Then, we see Him as the King of Love, weeping over sinners and pardoning them in His mercy. Finally, we see Him as the conqueror of sin and sorrow and death, with a crown of thorns on His brow, the Author of redemption, the Prince of our salvation. You think of Him as your priest, you think of Him as your prophet, but He wants you to know Him as your King— ruling over you, ruling in you, conquering for you and taking you to spread His kingdom abroad through the world.

Then, the coming of Christ to His kingdom, in this instance is the type of His coming to the individual heart. His ascension, His descent from the Mount of Olives and His entrance into Jerusalem, are the foreshadowing of that which has come to some of our hearts and which He wants to have come to all.

It is a glorious hour in the soul's life when a voice from heaven says: "Daughter of Zion, 'See, your king comes to you' " (Matthew 21:5). You never know the deep reality and the central fact of living Christianity until on the mountain you hear that voice: "See, your king comes to you." And, then, in your heart the sweet answering echo: "The LORD your God is with you, he is mighty to save" (Zephaniah 3:17). "Rejoice greatly, O daughter of Zion! . . . See, your king comes to you, righteous and having salvation" (Zechariah 9:9).

Is it true for you? Has the King come on His throne in your heart? Is Jesus, the Son of God, ruling in you in glory and royal majesty and supreme dominion? If He is, the world's glories are but a sham and mockery. Ambition cannot tempt you. Avarice cannot lead you aside. You have the King of kings within you, and you possess the reality of which all else is but the imitation.

I will never forget the day when across the face of these skies there was to me a living form, a real Christ—an everlasting friend who henceforth was no longer to be so far away that I had to pass through clouds and vast immensities to reach Him. But His throne was in the heart and His presence was within whispering distance. Oh, that today you might hear the voice that says: "Daughter of Zion, 'See, your king comes to you' " (Matthew 21:5). By and by, you will hear that other voice: "Daughter of Zion, your King comes for you."

These were the dying words of Frances Ridley Havergal, that glorious spirit who shone in the sky of Christian life for many years, as dear to many of us as if we had known her personally. When she passed away it seemed as though we had lost a personal friend. I like to trace the last moments of her life as she lay on that couch of pain and agony. Her face so lighted up that it was glorious. Her whole frame reached out and stretched forth as though to meet someone in mid air. At last the words breathed up from her parted lips: "My King, my King," and she took Him into her heart.

Will He ever come for you as a King? Do not be put off with the Christianity of mere church membership. Do not be mocked with the Christianity of mere baptism and confirmation and communion. Do not be satisfied with the mere hope of pardon and of heaven. Beloved, the true religion is Jesus within you, a living King and glorious Friend. May God grant that it may be true for you today: "The King comes to you."

Meek and Lowly

Again let me say before I leave it that you cannot have God come to you until you get like Him, meek and lowly. The King comes to you meek and lowly.

Now, some of you would not like to have Him come sitting on a donkey. If He would come in a carriage, ring the bell respectfully and have a good deal of show and social style, you would like it well. But I am afraid if Jesus were to ride upon a donkey to some of these mansions of Fifth Avenue, they would wonder who it was, and they would want Him to go around to the back door. They would not think that He was treating them with respect.

Now, if your King is going to come to you, He is not going to come to you with pride. Your King comes in such a way that you have to get down on your knees and meet something that brings real humiliation, that makes you very small. If you are not willing to get down and be loyal and take Christ as the meek and lowly One, He is not going to come to you. I have known some people who could never get God's full blessing until they let somebody bring it to them that they did not think much of. The Lord is going to come to you in this way. And if you will not let Him come thus, He has plenty of other places to go. Are you willing to have Him as your King on His own level?

Again, when He comes He will cleanse the temple. You must remember that He is going to control your heart and love. Have you offered and dedicated yourself to Him for this?

This is also the type of His coming to His work and His Church. He comes in great spiritual blessings, the outpouring of the Holy Spirit, the quickening of God's work and often in the new departure of the Church of God at such a time as this in our lives and history as a Church. Applying it to ourselves, we may look up and say: "Come, Lord Jesus, and take command of Your work. Be the Captain of Your host. Be the King of Your kingdom. Be the Proprietor of Your house. Be the Master of this work. Be the Beginning and the End, the All-in-all of Your people and all they desire to be, to have and do for You."

And I trust it is true of us today that the voices of the watchers are saying:

> Be not afraid, O land;
> be glad and rejoice.
> Surely the LORD has done great things.
> . . .
> rejoice in the LORD your God,

. . .
I will repay you for the years the
    locusts have eaten,

. . .
You will have plenty to eat, until you
    are full,
    and you will praise the name of the
    LORD your God,
    who has worked wonders for you;
    never again will my people be shamed.
        (Joel 2:21-26)

This is the type of His second coming, for that is what our hearts look forward to most of all in hope and watchful and earnest preparation. "See, your King comes to you," in a still grander sense. There is no coming of Christ to the heart, there is no coming of Christ to the Church, there is no coming of Christ to the world, that can satisfy the longing for His personal return. Some people will tell you that they have Him in their soul and that is enough. I find that the people who have Him in their soul long most for His nearer coming in the glorious advent.

There may be those to whom this is a new and somewhat unfamiliar thought. I will, therefore, just say in a few simple sentences that we believe the Scriptures to teach very plainly—and the number that so believe is increasing today in every part of the church—that the great hope of Christ's Church is His own personal advent. We believe in His own return in the flesh to this world again where He walked before for 33 years, and as He ascended to heaven, said: "I will come back and take you to be with me that you also may be where I am" (John 14:3). "This same Jesus, . . . will come back in the same way you have seen him go into heaven" (Acts 1:11).

The Dispensation of the Gentiles

We believe that this dispensation is the dispensation of the Gentiles, and that God is gathering in from the heathen nations a people for His kingdom. All that are willing to accept the gospel are accepted and pardoned and will have a share in the blessings of His kingdom. But He has nowhere said that during this age will the whole world be converted. The whole world is to hear the message, but only a portion will accept it. Many will be called, but few will be chosen, and yet all will be without excuse. When all have had an opportunity through the various tribes of earth, then we are told that the fullness of the Gentiles will have come in. Then the Lord will return and save His people, Israel, and give to the Jews again the hopes of their fathers and the salvation which they rejected when He was here on earth. At the same time, He Himself will return and reign over them, He will be the literal King of Zion, He will sit on the throne of His father, David, and His ancient followers will sit with Him ruling Israel.

This glorious day of the dear Lord's return is to be to us the day of the resurrection. It is to bring our return from the dust of death; or, if we are living at the time, it is to bring our translation into our resurrection bodies. It is to bring back our loved and lost who have died in Him, and it is to bring our own perfect spiritual and physical life. When He comes these bodies won't be feeble any more, but they will be immortal. These souls will be free and glorious and pure like His, and together we will meet Him and reign with Him on the earth for a thousand happy years.

That is the sure hope of the gospel and the promise of His Word. The conviction is pressing on Christians today that this advent is very near. That in the upheavals of society, in the workings of evil, in the intense unrest of the human heart, in the breaking up of nations and of social structures everywhere, in the throbbing of the world's heart in the earnest spirit of revival that is coming forth in the Church of God, in the love for His coming which is taking possession of the hearts of Christians, in strange manifestations of God's hand and power today in the healing of disease and the working of divine power in every part of the world—in these we are seeing the signs of a great crisis very near. The spaces are teeming with chariots and with horsemen, forms unseen are gathering, great armies are marshalling, and the trumpet of the great procession is sounding afar. A voice is beginning to say: "Here's the bridegroom! Come out to meet him!" (Matthew 25:6).

It is indeed a solemn age! I have not talked with an earnest man for several years but has said, "It is the most solemn age I ever knew of, and we are on the verge of a great and important change." I believe that the dear Lord is coming soon. Perhaps we have come with this work and into this place to be ready for His advent to prepare others to meet Him, and to spread abroad the message of His salvation and of His kingdom to all the world before He comes.

Now, it is for this that the Lord Jesus is calling you today. "See, your king comes to you." And, because He is coming, "the Lord needs [you]" (Matthew 21:5, 3).

The Lord's Instruments

Let us look a moment at the Lord's instruments, the persons and things He wants to use.   First, you notice He wanted a poor, blind beggar—poor Bartimeus was one of them of which He had need. Next, He sent two of His disciples before Him. Third, He needed a little colt—the humble foal of a donkey was His chief instrument, not the chariots and horsemen of Herod or Pilate, but a lowly little beast of burden, whom men only despised.

Again, He wanted the garments of the people to prepare for His coming. I believe when the Lord Jesus is coming, He wants poor, blind Bartimeus to tell the people that He is coming. He wants the blind and the dumb to speak for Him. He wants the two disciples—the lowly ones. He wants the little colt. And He wants your very robes to be ready and to be worthy of Him.

Again, He wanted the children as the instruments that were to share in His coming. The little ones were the voices raising the cry, "Hosanna!" And if we are to be used much to prepare for Christ's coming, we must gather the children.

Again, He wants the cry of poor sinners to herald His coming. This word "Hosanna" simply means the cry of the sinner. It means, "Have mercy on me." It is not hallelujah. That is a blessed cry. But hosanna is the very voice of a poor, guilty man. The Lord wants sinners by the thousands to throng at His feet and to prepare His way by their penitential tears, their cries for mercy and their songs of salvation. Jesus wants these things. He is in need of them—in need of the two disciples, in need of the little colt, in need of your garments, in need of your children, in need of poor sinners. If you today are a poor, lost man, the Lord has need of you. He is going to call somebody today that will be one of the glorious lamp-bearers in the procession of His advent. It seems to me if I were an unsaved sinner nothing would have more weight to lead me to Christ than this blessed thought that He will take me to be His servant and His helper. And so, today, if you have been living for self and sin, the Lord will take you this very moment, and, turning from Him, you can go forth as one of the heralders of His coming and one of the instruments to prepare for it.

Now, remember, dear friend, the Lord really needs you, for He would not say, unless He meant it, that He needs you and your services to prepare for His coming. The Lord needs people today who understand His gospel, He needs people who understand His coming, He needs people who love His coming, He needs people who labor for His coming. He needs your prayers, He needs your influence. In His mighty name would I throw this mighty word, for it seems to me it is just like a cord that should bind you to His altar—"The Lord needs you." I do not know where you are, but He needs you just there. I do not know what your station, but you are just in the place, in the situation, in which He needs you. He has adjusted your life for this very thing and put you in these very circumstances. He needed the Hebrew maid not in Israel, but in Syria, not as a daughter of Samaria at home, but as a poor captive abroad. So He needs you in your place, perhaps, as a helper in some position of humility.

He needed little Miriam just to come at the right moment. It may seem very little that you should teach a child, but one of those little ones may be the last great herald of the Master's coming. You do not know what He is going to do. He needs you.

It is so solemn for me to feel that He needs me just in the place He puts me and tells me to stand. Sometimes He gives demands and directions that seem a little strange and difficult, positions that require the crucifixion of one's self-consciousness, but if He needs you, there stand even if you stand alone. The Lord understands it. The Lord has need of you, and the Lord will stand for you.

He needs a little rivet just as much as a great

revolving wheel. Remember, the whole of life may hang on you. If we could only get men and women to understand that the whole framework of God's kingdom rests on each one's faithfulness. If they would come to their work, not saying this one or that one is going to pray, it will be all right, but saying, "If I fail, everything may fail; I am the very one called to hold up God's cause at this point. I must stand just as the soldier in that battlefield must stand, knowing that if he breaks the line the other lines may break." So the Lord has need of you today. Be careful, be faithful, and trust Him for evermore.

The Lord not only needs you, but He has a right to claim you. The Lord created you, made your body, made your soul for this very purpose—not to be indulged and admired, but because He needed you. Your very countenance, your very form, your very tone of voice, your very place in the family, your very social position, God gave you because He needed you. It belongs to Him. It is a part of His investment in you. It is a dreadful sacrilege to hold it back. The Lord not only created you, but He has provided for you, He has kept you, He has spent upon you more than anybody else ever spent, and He has a right to you. The Lord has redeemed you—bought you back. If you buy an article, you rather expect to get the good of it. If you buy a house, you do not expect anybody else to get the benefit of it. And so the Lord redeemed you for His own special use.

I would be ashamed to have my old father labor

for 20 years and work out his life and leave me his inheritance, and then take that money and squander it. Yes, I would be ashamed to take the blood of Christ to cover my sin or to save my wounded conscience, and prostitute it for sin. It is a horrible breach of trust. Give up the cross of Jesus if you are going to live for self and sin. Let Christ go. Just as soon take your mother's picture into that house of shame and hold it up to ridicule and derision as take the blood of Jesus into sin. It is too sacred. You were bought. You are not your own. The Lord has need of you and is expecting your service and has waited for it far too long already.

The Lord's Property

Not only has He redeemed you, but He owns you as His property. You say, "Well, I have not consecrated myself to God. I have not gone as far as these people. This man and that woman have consecrated themselves, and I expect a good deal of them." Oh, dear soul, Christ consecrated you when He died for you. You are as much His own as if you had given yourself. The only difference is, the other has recognized the claim and you have not. But you are His; you belong to Him. You are not your own, and that does not lessen your obligation. The Lord has claims upon you. It is a very touching thought to me that He has made us the members by which He is to do His own work. He has made us the instruments of conveying His great gifts to the world, and He does not seem to have any other way to communicate Himself fully except through you. You just stand in the position of being Christ's hands, and feet, and tongue and limbs. He is the Head and you are the body.

Now, suppose my head and heart wanted to do certain things, but my hands would not obey. Suppose my feet would not go forth on those errands. Suppose that I was all paralyzed or divided up, or selfish, and would not obey the voice of my brain. What a strange, distorted life I would have. Now, that is just the way our dear Lord is. He is our Head and we are His hands. He wants you to be a blessing to the world, and if you will not, He is hindered by His very own flesh and blood.

Imagine that you were a trustee appointed for the special care of a sum of money which was to be for the benefit of poor children and some good-hearted friend had put a million dollars in your hands. Imagine that you used it for yourself. How his heart would regret that he had given you this trust and let his kind purpose be hindered by your faithlessness. You and I are the executors of His blessing. If we do not obey Him, when we meet Him at the last He will hold us responsible for the souls that are lost and for our failure to carry out the purpose of His blessing. He needs you and me. I trust that over you will hang a spell thrown from the Eternal, thrown over you from the cross where He died, thrown over you from the heaven where He abides, thrown over you from the judgment seat where you will give your account. The Lord needs you. He wants you to begin today and work for the Lord's coming. He sends you forth, saying: "Loose that little colt that is tied. Set free that influence that is bound up. The Lord has need of it." He puts His hand on your shoulder, and you cannot be released.

May God help you to be true, for it is sad when we disobey the claim of God. The barren fig tree was needed, but it would not give Him any fruit. The Lord needed the fruit of that tree, but it refused Him its fruit. And what was the consequence? Before another day had come it was withered. And so, beloved, if the Lord has need of you and you do not meet Him, He will wither you, too, and you will stand like that barren tree.

There are lives, I know, today, that do not know what is the matter—all blasted, all barren, all joyless, because when the Lord needed them they were afraid to obey. They refused to step out, and the Lord has no more use for them. The Lord will excuse you if you want to be excused. When Elijah went to anoint Elisha to be a prophet, Elisha said, "Let me kiss my father and mother good-by" (1 Kings 19:20). And Elijah said, "Go back . . . what have I done to you?" (19:20). It was as if he had said, "It does not matter. If you do not mind, God does not mind. You can be excused." Elisha went and took his oxen and his plow and offered them up in sacrifice to his God, lest he should be tempted to go back again—he gave the whole thing over to God—and was henceforth known as the man who poured water on the hands of Elijah. "The Lord needs [you]" (Matthew 21:3), but if you want to be excused, He may say, "Go, return. What have I done to you? I will call somebody else." But oh, I should not like to be excused.

And oh, the blessedness, on the other hand, of being used by God; the sweetness of that consciousness that the Lord did take us and make something of us. I have seen in a museum a drinking cup of George Washington. How it was treasured because he drank water out of it. Perhaps it is the pen of some martyr or the ink bottle of some reformer. By and by they will come again in heaven and say, "The Lord used her; the Lord used him"; and you will be forever glorious because God made you His instrument. It is glorious to be used by God.

Once, away in the Highlands of Scotland, Queen Victoria, while walking in the country near her summer palace, sat down in an old Highland lady's cabin and began to talk to her. She sat down on a little, old, three-legged stool and talked away for a long time with the old granny. However, she did not let her know who she was. After she said good-bye and left, the old lady wondered at her generosity. A few hours afterward, somebody came in and said, "Do you know who that was?" "No," she said. "Why, that was the queen." "The queen! Did she sit on my stool?" And then she took up that stool and put it in a secret place by itself and curtained it around. When people asked her why, she said, "Nobody will ever sit on that stool again." She handed it down to her children because her queen had sat upon it. I guess if the

Roman Catholic Church, or the old Medieval Church, could have gotten the bones of that little colt that Christ sat upon, they would have built a church somewhere in Italy for it. It was not necessary that that little colt should ever drive the plow any more. It was not necessary that it should ever drag a cart. It had done its mission. The Lord had need of it. He used it, and forevermore it was linked with Him.

Oh, beloved, let the Lord use you and you will be glorious forevermore. Go today and ask, "Lord, do You want me for this work, or do You want me for some work that perhaps I would not have chosen myself? Here I am, Lord. You have need of me, and oh, I have greater need of You." And when He comes you will find ten thousandfold return for the sacrifices and services of these days. With our faces, then, toward His second coming, let us go forth and let Him use us as He will, and then give us a place by His side upon His throne. To Jesus, our King, be the glory forever and ever. Amen.

CHAPTER 5

Partnership with God

We are God's fellow workers. (1 Corinthians 3:9)

The members of an English publishing firm sat down together at their annual dinner in Exeter Hall. There were more than 2,000 partners at the table. It was a strange sight to look at that immense crowd of men and realize that they were one firm. They had adopted the plan of making all their employees partners, and it had worked most successfully.

That picture leads our thoughts to a higher relationship. Our work for God is a great partnership. "We are God's fellow workers." When the Lord Jesus was on earth, He always declared that His work was done in partnership with His Father. "My father is always at his work to this very day, and I, too, am working" (John 5:17). "It is the Father living in me, who is doing his work" (14:10). And He taught His disciples that their work must be in similar partnership with Him. "Anyone who has faith in me will do what I have been doing. He will do even greater things than these" (14:12). And when He left them, Mark gives us this last picture of His ascension: "He was taken up into heaven and he sat at the right hand of God. Then the disciples went out and preached everywhere, and the Lord worked with them and confirmed his word by the signs that accompanied it" (Mark 16:19-20).

Let us look at the two sides of this partnership:

God's Part

1. He pays our debts and establishes our credit.

He finds the firm insolvent and ruined, and not only so, but also criminal. And He pays all the old obligations and puts all His own credit to its account, making our standing as good as His own, even in the sight of God.

A friend of mine once told me of a businessman he knew who had a dishonest clerk. The man embezzled considerable sums of money from him, but at last was brought to repentance and became a true Christian. He came to his employer, after a great struggle, to confess his wrong, expecting not only dismissal, but perhaps also severe punishment. The merchant heard his story and was deeply moved, for he knew that he might easily have escaped detection. The contrite clerk closed by saying, "Of course I cannot expect that you will ever employ me as a servant again." At that, the businessman replied, "No, I never can employ you as a servant again. But you shall be a partner in my business, for I know the worth of such a testimony as that you have just given."

Not often does man act so nobly, but this is just what God has done. He has assumed our liabilities, has canceled our crimes, has even suffered their consequences Himself and has also taken us into His own complete fellowship and made us joint heirs in all His riches of grace and glory.

2. He supplies all the resources and capital of the business.

He does not send us, like Pharaoh's task-masters, to work without materials, but He invests all the resources that we need, Himself. He does not even limit our capital, but says to us, "God is able to make all grace abound to you, so that in all at all times, having all that you need, you will abound in every good work" (2 Corinthians 9:8).

We often see after the titles of business corporations the word "Limited." But there is no such condition upon our incorporation in the service of God. It is all grace, always, all that you need, in every good work. Our service is not to be measured, therefore, by our natural talents, our narrow sphere or any condition. We can draw of Him to any extent for His work. A wealthy merchant said once to a dear servant of God, "Draw on me any time you need, for it will be hon-

ored." So God says to His workers, "Where
natural strength fails, and natural talent is insufficient, My power and My wisdom meet all demands." When you have to cry, "We have no
power to face this vast army that is attacking us.
We do not know what to do" (2 Chronicles
20:12), then remember, "the LORD, . . . the Creator of the ends of the earth. He will not grow
tired or weary, and his understanding no one
can fathom" (Isaiah 40:28). When nature cries,
"We are not sufficient to claim anything for ourselves," faith can answer, "But our competence
comes from God. He has made us competent as
ministers of a new covenant" (2 Corinthians 3:5-
6).

3. He entrusts to us the chief work of His kingdom.

He does not do it Himself and leave us simply
to gather up the fragments, but He Himself does
all that is difficult and trying, leaving us the joy of
harvest.

Down into the wild wilderness He came and
cleaned the ground and prepared the soil with
toil and pain. Then to us He left the delightful
task of rearing the fruits and harvesting His hus-
bandry. He is the strong vine, sending out its
roots into the deep places of strength and life
and supporting all the branches. But to us, the
branches, He gives the joy and riches of bearing
the fruit. He spent 33 years amid the shame and
toil of the workshop, the judgment hall and the
cross. When it was over He had less than a thou-

sand followers in all the world. To His disciples He gave thousands of souls in the first month after His ascension. "He will do even greater things than these," He says, "because I am going to the Father" (John 14:12). To us He has given these greater works. Angels would be glad to do them, but mortals are privileged instead.

4. He prepares the workers.

All true workers must be prepared. The learning of a valuable business or art is no small advantage in secular affairs. For His service our Master Himself prepares His workers. "For we are God's workmanship, created in Christ Jesus to do good works" (Ephesians 2:10).

We are made with a special view to this very thing, that we may be adapted to good works. Adaptation is necessary in everything. Without it the fish is lost on the land and the fowl in the sea and the quadruped in the air. Each has its natural element and action, and this is easy and spontaneous. The organ is adapted for music, and the orange tree for fruit bearing, and the rose for sweet perfume. To try to make a rose grow oranges, and an organ act as a locomotive, would be foolish and idle business. And so, to expect an unregenerate soul to do Christ's service is vain. It succeeds as well as a blacksmith would at a surgical operation, or a ploughman at a fresco painting. Therefore, Christ prepares His instruments. He makes them for this very end. He puts into them the instincts, impulses and endowments that will lead them to choose, to love and to accomplish the results intended. And He especially fits each one for the service assigned. Fitly framed together, they severally fulfill their respective relationships and spheres. Each of us is created, regenerated and divinely educated for the very place we are called to fill.

The great author of our spiritual training and the source of our power is the Holy Spirit. He is promised to every true servant of Christ as a "spirit of power, of love and of self-discipline" (2 Timothy 1:7).

Without Him and His gifts we can do nothing acceptable to God or effectual with men. He must open to us the Scriptures, by which "the man of God may be thoroughly equipped for every good work" (3:17). He must lead us into the separation and sanctification in which we will be "useful to the Master and prepared to do any good work" (2:21). He must reveal to us the things of God which are spiritually discerned and speak through us "with a demonstration of the Spirit's power" (1 Corinthians 2:4), or our words shall be idle and vain. And He does prepare His "chosen vessels" and his "polished shafts," and make them "have divine power to demolish strongholds" (2 Corinthians 10:4).

5. He prepares the works we will do.

He not only prepares the instruments, but He also prepares the works. Paul tells us that we are, "created in Christ Jesus to do good works, which

God prepared in advance for us to do" (Ephesians 2:10). Our works are prepared for us, and we have only to do them. This is an unspeakable comfort. We don't have to make them, but to receive them and wear them as habits and garments.

In a drama the actors may have to wear a great many different costumes, but they do not need to make them. They are provided for the piece; they have only to put them on and wear them in the proper place. At one time it is the part of a workman, at another a merchant, at another a prince. But the proper robe for each is provided, and they have only to put it on and wear it.

So the Lord Jesus prepares our work for us. At one time we need the garment of love, at another power, at another wisdom. At other times we must understand a human heart, or weep with a mourner, or warm a hardened heart, or cheer a depressed one. Sometimes we must lead one to the Savior, or the Sanctifier, or the Healer. We might have to meet some perplexing issue or decision at some great turning point in life. But all is ready, laid up for us in Christ our Lord, needing only to be transferred into our life in action and experience. So that in the service, as much as in the experience, it is "I no longer live, but Christ lives in me" (Galatians 2:20). They are not our works, but His works in us. We are the pen, and He is the Hand that guides it. We are only the voice, He is the Work that speaks by it. We are only the vessel, and He is the precious Living Water that fills it. This makes our work so easy.

Spontaneous service is the overflow of the heart. John Bunyan says of his book: "I wrote because joy did make me write." So Jesus says of true service in the Spirit: "Streams of living water will flow from within him" (John 7:38). Most persons find their work a burden. The true servant of Christ finds the Lord carries both him and his burden, too. We begin our work for the Lord with great zeal and try to help the Lord and His cause. At the last we feel that He needs not us or our eager impetuousness, and we are glad to lay the burdens of His work on Him.

A little child insisted on carrying an armful of his father's books up the stairs. The father told him the load was too heavy, but the little fellow insisted and started with his load. By and by they came tumbling down in confusion, and he burst into tears and stretched out his tired hands to his father for help. The father took him in his arms, and then lifted the books and carried them, too. So He takes us and our service, and we serve Him best when we rest upon His breast and just let Him use us as He needs us and fills us. The disciples thought they could keep and manage Him when they took Him from His weary toil and put Him on a pillow in the back of the ship to sleep. But they were glad to put themselves in His care before long and awake Him to save them from destruction. Such service is as strong as it is calm. It moves with the mighty tides of heaven. "I labor," Paul says concerning it, "struggling with all his energy, which so powerfully works in me" (Colossians 1:29).

6. *He rewards the work.*

He rewards the work and shares the recompense with us as fully as if we had done it all. "Even now the reaper draws his wages, even now he harvests the crop for eternal life" (John 4:36). I cannot tell you what that reward will be. But even here you and I know something of the joy of bringing a soul to Jesus. We know something of what it means to have someone meet us in after years and tell us how some word or prayer of ours had once helped or saved them. Oh, what will it be, in heaven, to find them coming from the east and the west, bringing the souls they have won, and recognize us as the instrument of all their blessing. To hear Him say: "Whatever you did for one of the least of these brothers of mine, you did for me" (Matthew 25:40). "He will dress himself to serve, will have them recline at the table and will come and wait on them" (Luke 12:37). "Those who are wise will shine . . . like the stars for ever and ever" (Daniel 12:3). They will be rulers over many things and will enter into the joy of their Lord. They will share His kingdom and His throne and be promoted to grander service through the millennial years. Oh, then we will not regret the nights of watching and days of toil, but wish we could have done and suffered more for so great and far-surpassing a reward.

Our Part

1. To recognize the work as His.

A great deal of Christian work is our work, and He is only consulted and asked to help it. True Christian service is given to Him and done as His and at His bidding and under His absolute responsibility and ownership. It should not be, "What am I doing for the Lord?" but, "What is the Lord doing through me?"

Let us consecrate our work as well as ourselves. Then we will not hear so much about our church, our connection, our cause and our work, by like the men of old, will "dwell with the king for his work."

2. To recognize the necessity and obligation of our coworking.

God could do without us. He could, by His direct omnipotence, Himself do all He uses us to do. But He has appointed human agency in the salvation of men. He has arranged for the supply of the world with the Living Water by the pipes and channels of our hearts and hands. And, therefore, if we fail to do our part, there is a failure in the supply. What a grief it must be to Him to know that there is enough in the resources of redemption for all mankind, and that it cost Him His lifeblood. And yet, through the unfaithfulness of His servants, so many are left to perish without it. We are members of Christ. But just as we have seen a large and generous heart and a gifted head hampered by a debilitated body and hindered in carrying out its noble aims and purposed by paralyzed limbs, so often Christ looks in vain for hands and hearts to carry out His merciful and mighty plans for a lost world.

He has so ordered it that His grace must reach others through us. It is a great crime against His love as well as against the souls of men to fail to work together with Him. It is as great a crime as it would be for a generous benefactor to leave a large inheritance to the poor children of the city and deposit it with certain trustees for this end, and these trustees, instead of giving it to the persons for whom it was intended, should spend it on themselves and let the children starve in neglect. Do we realize that we are His trustees, His representatives, His agents, His body, His hands and feet and voice, through whom He has condescended to work? Will we not be true to our glorious Head and the trust that He has given us?

3. To work in His way and plan.

Much work is destroyed by being done in our way. He demands that if we build in His temple, we must build on His plan, on the foundation He has laid according to His specifications and with the materials He has supplied. "See that you make them according to the pattern shown you on the mountain" (Exodus 25:40). "Teaching them to obey everything I have commanded you" (Matthew 28:20).

We often hear of some new religious "enterprise" being started. The church is not an "enterprise," but a divine temple built of divine materials by the Holy Spirit through consecrated men and women. There is too much of man's "enterprise" about it. Instead of the simplicity of the gospel, the power of the Spirit, the agency of truth, faith and prayer, the personal holiness of a consecrated membership, the testimony of people separated from the world, the power of personal work for souls, an open door for the poor and lost, an aggressive work to reach the outcast and hopeless, the free and voluntary gifts of God's children, a full gospel for spirit, soul and body and a church of which a living Christ is the Life and Lord—instead of these we have smart preachers and fashionable people, operatic choirs and ungodly trustees, church fairs and Sunday school theatricals, religious concerts and charity balls, splendid church edifices and vast religious endowments, pew rents which exclude the poor, philosophical essays which exclude the gospel and the Savior, culture and scholasticism which leave out the Holy Spirit and a mass of man's machinery which leaves little room for the supernatural operation or the power of the Living God. The work of the apostles was under the direction of the Holy Spirit. Natural gifts were not despised, but all was fused into the living fire of the Spirit of power and consecration. The planting to Christianity in the

continent of Africa was wholly due to the obedience of Philip to the Holy Spirit, bidding him
leave a great work in Samaria and go down into
the desert. The result was the conversion of the
Prince of Ethiopia and the first spread of the gospel among the Gentile nations. The planting of
the gospel in Europe was also due to the obedience of Paul to the guidance of the Holy Spirit,
forbidding him to preach in Asia and Bythinia,
and calling him to Macedonia. The same God is
with us still, and if we would let Him lead us, we
would see the same glorious results.

4. To work in His strength.

The reason why civilized nations are in advance
of barbarous people is because they have learned
the secrets of nature and know how to use the hidden forces of God. The savage needs a hundred
men to drag the load which an American engineer
can carry with a touch on the valve of his steam
engine. The one uses his own strength, the other
the hidden forces of nature. The mighty forces of
electricity and steam are only God's power taken
into partnership with man for his secular work. So
we can take His power into partnership for spiritual work. And, instead of the toil and strain of
our own wisdom and skill, we can put on His
strength and use His omnipotence. A touch of
God's hand is worth a million human hands.

A company of engineers was lifting an immense
and costly obelisk to its pedestal in Alexandria.
They had raised it aloft, almost to the level of the

vase. But it needed one inch more to clear and swing in upon its pediment. The ropes had been strained to their utmost tension and nothing more could be done without lowering the whole pulleys and mechanism and commencing over. There was a moment of intense disappointment. Man's power could do no more. Suddenly a sailor's voice rang out clear and sharp: "Wet the ropes." In an instant the engineer understood the simple hint. The ropes were saturated with water from top to bottom. In a few moments the immense obelisk began to rise, slowly, surely, silently. It reached the level of the base. It passed it and swung clear, settling in its place. The cords were loosed; it stood firm and steady on its foundation and a shout of cheers went up from a thousand voices at the simple touch of power that came forth from nature at a word.

So is the work of God. There is a limit where all our strength comes to an end. The might of a million men cannot go farther, but there is a secret place of power, and one whisper of faith will bring omnipotence so simply, so silently, so easily, yet so victoriously, that earth and heaven will shout the glad notes of praise forever. This is the secret of the work. "You will receive power when the Holy Spirit comes on you; and you will be my witnesses . . . to the ends of the earth" (Acts 1:8). It is the same old gospel. Let us put it into our work as well as our souls, and we will find that He is All in all.

CHAPTER 6

Words for Discouraged Workers

Run, tell that young man, "Jerusalem will be a city without walls because of the great number of men and livestock in it. And I myself will be a wall of fire around it," declares the LORD, "and I will be its glory within." (Zechariah 2:4-5)

Zechariah, a young man, who perhaps at the time of this Scripture was just beginning his prophetic ministry, began his ministry in the eighth month, and in the 11th month of the same year he gave the next series of visions. So you see there was a great deal done between the eighth and the 11th month. God compressed a great deal into a small space when His people were ready for it.

Let us look at some of the messages of
Zechariah. The first message that Zechariah gave
to the people was not exactly one of reproof, but it
was a gentle reminder of the warnings which had
already been given and a very serious caution not
to forget them.

But he does not linger long over the words of
reproof. He just touches the canvas with a mere
outline of the vision of judgment that, like a de-
parting cloud, has gone and will never come again
if they are faithful. Then he presses on to that
which is bright and hopeful. In a series of seven
visions Zechariah gives them a succession of pictures of hope and cheer like, perhaps, nothing else
in the sacred volume for beauty and encouraging
power.

They all came on the same night. It took many
hours to record them and many years to fulfill
them. But they all came to the mind of this young
man perhaps in a single hour. On the 24th day of
the 11th month, very near the close of the year,
when sleep perhaps was beginning to throw its
veil over his brain, there rose before him a pano-
rama of strange scenes, peopled with moving
forms from the heavenly world. Voices fell upon
his ear, and God covered him with the cloud of
His presence, and out of the glory came these
wonderful visions.

Encouragement Against Their Depression

The first was a vision of a low bottom, something like the banks of the river Nile, or the low

banks of the Kedron, and on this low land were growing groves of myrtle trees. It looked something like a city of the dead, for the myrtle was the tree of sorrow. As he looked upon the scene, the low valley and the dark green myrtle branches, the type of his people's sorrow and sadness, he saw in the midst of them a number of war horses of different colors with heavenly horsemen seated upon them. He asked who they were. The answer came that these were God's messengers whom He had sent abroad throughout the earth.

As he watched, he saw another form, no longer as angel, but the Angel of the Covenant Himself— the Son of God. There in the midst of this dark, sad scene, beside these angel horsemen he saw Jesus Christ, the Angel of the Covenant. The Angel lifted His voice to heaven and began to pray for His suffering people. "LORD Almighty, how long will you withhold mercy from Jerusalem and from the towns of Judah, which you have been angry with these seventy years?" (Zechariah 1:12)—the 70 years of the captivity.

It was Jesus praying for His people. It was the Great High Priest beginning His intercession for you and for me. Others had prayed, but there had not come any answer. But then Jesus clasped His hands and looked up to His Father. He uttered just one prayer to God, and the shadow of 70 years passed away; the clouds were all broken. And the next verse contains the answer: "So the LORD spoke kind and comforting words to the angel who talked with me" (1:13).

The Father cannot turn away the pleadings of His Son. One prayer of Jesus is worth a million of the best prayers on earth. If you want to get your prayers answered, get Him to pray for you. All the years of this restoration began with that little prayer of Jesus to His Father. And is it not glorious to know today that He "lives to intercede for [us]" (Hebrews 7:25)? For we have a great High Priest who has passed into the heavens—Jesus the Son of God. "Let us then approach the throne of grace with confidence, so that we may receive mercy and find grace to help us in our time of need" (4:16).

Then the answer goes on: "Proclaim this word: This is what the LORD Almighty says: 'I am very jealous for Jerusalem and Zion, ... I will return to Jerusalem with mercy, . . . My towns will again overflow with prosperity, and the LORD will again comfort Zion and choose Jerusalem' " (Zechariah 1:14-17).

That is the first vision. It is the vision of the sorrow and depression of God's people—among the myrtle trees, in the bottom, low down and covering themselves with sorrow, with God's mighty angels moving among them, God's dear Son praying for them, and God answering: "I will return with mercy."

Encouragement Against Their Enemies

We come now to the second vision. "Then I looked up—and there before me were four horns!" (1:18). He knew what they meant. They were the symbols of those cruel earthly powers that had pushed against Judah and Jerusalem and pierced her heart and crushed her under their ruthless feet. They were the horns of earthly power, the figure by which God always represents the evil powers of the world. But he said: "Then the LORD showed me four craftsmen" (1:20), with saw and hatchet and plane, coming to meet and fray these sharp horns. "I asked, 'What are these coming to do?' He answered, 'These are the horns that scattered Judah so that no one could raise his head' " (1:20-21)—that is to peel them down and take the sharp points from them, to soften them as you would soften the end of a broom, so that they should have no power to harm.

This second vision means defense against the hostility of enemies. The four horns mean that there are enemies on all sides—north and south, and east and west. Look where you will there are horns, but look where you will there are craftsmen to meet them. There is just as much protection as there is opposition, and greater is He that is for us than all they that are against us. Cheer up then, again, beloved. Do not mind the horns, but remember God has got His tools to take their sharpness all away. No harm can come to those that serve and follow Him. "I will contend with those who contend with you, and your children I will save" (Isaiah 49:25).

Encouragement Against the Smallness of Their Numbers

Then we have the third vision. He saw a

young man with a measuring line in his hand, and he was very busy and important. He was a contractor, or a clerk of work, or some official in connection with building operations. He had a long tape in his hand, and was measuring off the ground. Zechariah came up to him and said: "Where are you going?" (Zechariah 2:2). And he answered: "To measure Jerusalem, to find out how wide and how long it is. [We are going to build walls, and we want to lay out the work]" (2:2). And then there came a voice from the angel: "Run, tell that young man that is laying out the work and mea-suring off the ground for the walls to stop. Tell him there is no need for his measuring line. Tell him there is no need for his work. Tell him that God is undertaking the business and is going to build all the walls Himself, and man's measuring line is too short for God's plan. Tell this young man that his ideas are too small and too petty for this great work. Tell him that Jerusalem will be inhabited as towns without walls by a multitude of men and cattle."

You are going to make a little town for thousands of people, and God is going to have millions of people. And when He gets them together He says: "I myself will be a wall of fire around it, . . . and I will be its glory within" (2:5). What a glorious promise! What a glorious reproof to our little faith! Man is always getting his hand on the work in some little way, and God is always waiting to get us out of the way, so that He may do larger things for us. Their enemies were saying: "What is the use of building Jerusalem? Where are you going to get your people? You have only got a little handful there. Your building of this temple for a few hundred people is all nonsense." They had only 50,000. There used to be 9,000,000, and 50,000 was a very small nation compared with 9,000,000. It would not make one good-sized city.

They were all discouraged about their small numbers, and this vision came to encourage them in this respect. It came to tell them that God had the people in His hand like the sands of the sea and the stars in the heavens—if they only had faith enough to rise to His perfect will, then He would protect them and guard them Himself. And just as the shepherd builds his wall of fire round his folds at night, and it is better than any wall of masonry to keep the wolves out, so God will shine forth in their midst with His fiery presence. Next He added: "Whoever touches you touches the apple of [my] eye" (2:8). So that as your eyelids fall when a grain of dust comes near, or when a sandfly touches against the tender organs of sight, down comes that little trap door and shuts out the intruder—so God says He will be just as sensitive to your dangers. Then He added: "Many nations will be joined with the LORD in that day and will become my people" (2:11).

Beloved, is not that a good and comforting word for us—a little band thinking sometimes about our lack of power and numbers? But God says if we will trust Him we will not need any measuring line. I have always been afraid to number people. I used to be able to tell just how many I had on the communion roll and how many I had talked with about salvation. But since God has called me to this work, I have kept no figures except such as are necessary for church order. I do not know how many I have talked with. I do not know how many I have prayed with. When I try to use the measuring line, God seems to say, "My child, let me bless without measure." If we can humble ourselves enough to forget the numbers, if we can stop man's glorying, and sitting at the feet of Jesus see Him only and glorify Him only, God will see that His promises are "immeasurably more than all we ask or imagine" (Ephesians 3:20).

Encouragement Against Conscious Unworthiness

Now we come to the fourth vision. The people took courage from these blessed words and went on with their work. The temple was at last so far finished that they were ready to worship in it, and they came through the person of Joshua to worship before the Lord. But they had no sooner come there than on the right hand of Joshua there came another character. "Joshua . . . standing before the angel of the LORD, and Satan standing at his right side to accuse him" (Zechariah 3:1).

There he was pointing with his finger to poor Joshua, who was covered with filthy garments, and looking up to God as much as to say: "This is a pretty sight in Your holy temple, to see this man here, representing the nation, defiled with sin and unfit to appear before You." That is just what Satan always does. His very name means "the accuser." His business is to point his finger at your filthy garments and remind you of your unworthiness. Sometimes you will find him standing at your right hand in the very house of God to accuse you. How often, when some work for God has been laid upon you, has he come to you and with his foul whisper said: "You are not fit for this?" How often, when you have wished to speak to someone, has he come to you to re-press you with the reminder of something that is lacking in yourself? How often, when you kneel in prayer to ask great things of God, has he said to you: "How dare you claim this with your un-worthiness?" And so he holds you back and keeps you down.

What did Joshua do? He could not do anything. He knew that the filthy garments belonged to him—only too well he knew it. But oh, the blessed Lord stepped in and answered for him, and said unto Satan, without giving Joshua time to answer or even to get confused: "The LORD rebuke you, Satan! The LORD, who has chosen Jerusalem, re-buke you!" (3:2). "Is not it enough that I have cho-sen them, and that they are like brands plucked from the burning fire? But they are not in it now. I have torn them out and saved them. Though they have the mark of the flames upon them they are mine, and I have chosen them." Then God made the answer more emphatic still: "Take off his filthy clothes" (3:4). Next He added: "See, I

have taken away your sin, and I will put rich garments on you" (3:4). And so God took off his old
robes, covered him with the beauty of Jesus, and
then He said: "Put a clean turban on his head"
(3:5). And they set a fair diadem on his head and
crowned him as an accepted king and a pure
priest, a holy worshiper through the Lord Jesus
Christ.

That is the way God will comfort you when the
enemy reminds you of all your imperfections if
you will put them away with a true heart and take
Jesus for your righteousness. The Lord does not
merely accept you, but He crowns you with His
blessing. He says those great words: "If you will
walk in my ways and keep my requirements, then
you will govern my house and have charge of my
courts, and I will give you a place among these
standing here" (3:7). He says to us: "I will give
you a place of honor even among the heavenly
thrones. Sinner though you were, I now cover you
with My beauty and glory through My precious
blood."

Provision for Their Weakness

They were conscious of being very weak. It is a
very sad thing to be without human power and
also without divine power. And that was their position. So a fifth vision came. This figure repre-
sented God's strength in their weakness.
Zechariah beheld a golden, seven-branch candlestick, and on each side of this sevenfold lamp there
was a living olive tree. As the olive tree grew and

ripened its berries, he saw the berries pressed out—not by hands of men, but by some unseen force—and their oil poured into a pipe which connected the tree with the lamp. They were pouring in their oil as fast as they made it, and so kept the lamp burning without the touch of human hand—without the least human machinery.

I do not know anything so exquisite and delicate in the imagery of the Bible. Zechariah looked with wondering eyes and remembered how the temple had to be supplied with oil by snuffers and vessels and the hands of 30,000 Levites. He asked: "What are these, my lord?" (4:4). And the answer came back: " 'Not by might nor by power, but by my Spirit,' says the LORD Almighty" (4:6).

That is the way the work is going to be carried on. This is God's candlestick, the true church of Jesus Christ. It is not going to be supplied by man's wisdom, but the Holy Spirit is going to be its life and invisible power. On each side of His church there are two living trees, one of them on the heaven side, the other on the earth side. The one on the heaven side is Jesus, the High Priest; the one on the earth side is the Holy Spirit who dwells within us. And so we stand between the two—Jesus on one side, the Spirit on the other side—both of them, with living and constant supply, pouring into us their very life, and keeping the lamp burning " 'Not by might nor by power, but by my Spirit,' says the LORD Almighty."

Beloved, that is God's way of nurturing His church. God wants man's hands put aside. Just as the measuring line must go, so must the snuffers and the tunnels go, too. God must be constantly breathing life to the throbbing pulses of the church that He has redeemed and loved. But then He added: "What are you, O mighty mountain? . . . you will become level ground. Then he will bring out the capstone to shouts of 'God bless it! God bless it!' " (4:7). Not man's doings, but all Christ's. And the work will be finished. Then He added: "Who despises the day of small things?" (4:10). That is just the day that God uses and blesses.

I remember well the cold and desolate afternoon, years ago, when a little band of humble, praying Christians met in an upper room to begin this work for God (the Gospel Tabernacle in New York City, which eventually was the beginnings of The Christian and Missionary Alliance). There were less than a dozen, and we asked the Lord to give us His Word for this work. We opened our Bibles, and these words were just before us: "Who despises the day of small things? . . . 'Not by might nor by power, but by my Spirit', says the LORD Almighty." We knelt before Him there and thanked Him that we were poor, and thanked Him that we were few, and thanked Him that we were weak. We threw ourselves upon the might of the Holy Spirit, and He has never failed us. If we keep little enough, and lowly enough, and humble enough, and trustful enough, He will love and bless us more and more. Oh, beloved, cherish this vision! I know God wants us to remember in our work, above everything else, the might of weakness which is the might of God.

Defense Against Iniquity in Their Midst

The fifth chapter gives us the next vision. He saw a flying roll, with curses written on it, touching the house of this one and that one as it passed by. He asked: "What does this mean?" The answer came: "This is God's curse that strikes the willful and wicked" (author's loose paraphrase of 5:2-3). You do not need to curse anybody. God will judge. If men and women will sin and go on unrepentant, God has His flying scroll.

Then, in the same vision, He saw an ephah (a measuring basket), and in it a woman's form as the type of iniquity. And he saw two angels take the measure and put the lid upon her head and shut her down in the measure, and then carry it away to the land of Babylon, putting it in its own place. He asked again: "What does this mean?" And the answer was: "God is going to take the evil away Himself in that way. He is going to smite that which will not turn to Him. Then He is going to lift up and turn out of your midst all that offends, and put it out of your way, so that you do not need to do anything but trust Him. And God will keep His work pure." That was their fear. They asked: "How can we be sure that we will not be hindered by elements coming in among us that are not pure?" He said: "God will do that Himself." And so, beloved, we will take God to guard the purity of His work.

How wonderfully has He guarded and kept us. How many times it has seemed that evil and dangerous elements were trying to break in. But God, without any human contrivance, almost without speaking a word, has just kept us; and, as we trusted Him, guarded His work making it simple, and scriptural, and heavenly, and holy, so that He can bless us to the fullness of His love and will.

Defense Against the Powers of the World

In the next vision, "I looked up again—and there before me were four chariots" (Zechariah 6:1). These four chariots were going out in different directions. One was coming north, another was following after it. Another was going south, and another was following in its train.

He asked: "What are these, my lord?" (6:4). And the Lord said: "These are the four spirits of heaven, going out from standing in the presence of the Lord of the whole world" (6:5). One was going away north into the Grecian empire; the other was going away south into the Persian, for these were the two great empires of that day. And He said: "Those going toward the north country have given my Spirit rest in the land of the north" (6:8). That is, they have taken My powers with them to hold in check all evil that would hinder My kingdom. And so you need not fear the power of the northern kingdom or the southern throne. I have got armies there who are encamping in the clouds and around about the thrones and camps of earth. And you need not fear.

And today God says to you and me that He has His chariots in the north, and in the south, and in all lands. He is overturning, restraining and controlling all things for the glory of His name and for the advancement of His church. Remember this vision of providence and of God's controlling power in all human affairs, and be sure the wrath of man will praise Him and the remainder thereof will be restrained. God wants us to take the place of faith and know that at the throne of prayer we can touch the mightier hands, and thus bring about the coming of the Messiah.

These are the seven visions which Zechariah saw. As he closed them, he added another beautiful incident, with which we will close. It is the last incident in the sixth chapter. It is one of exceeding beauty, and very comforting, I think, to us today. Just at this time there came a little deputation from Babylon, from the captives that had not returned to Jerusalem, and they brought along with them some presents of silver and of gold. Though they could not return, they sent what they could to help. From afar their gifts were carried by the living hands of these three men—Heldai, Tobijah and Jedaiah. They brought their money to Joshua. As soon as it was received, God spoke through Zechariah, and gave this direction: "Take this money that these men have brought. God does not need it in His temple, because He has all the money. What God wants is their love. But take the money that they have brought and forge it into crowns, and then take the crowns and put them on the head of Joshua, the high priest. Let him wear them there on the day of some public service in the temple of the Lord. And let him tell the people and you tell them, Zechariah, that he is but the type of another great One who is to bear the same name. Tell them that there is another Joshua coming—Jesus of Nazareth, that He is to be the great High Priest. That just as Joshua wears the silver and gold for a crown, so the day is coming when Jesus will take the gifts of His people, the little sacrifices that they have brought, and make them into crowns. He will wear them on His head before all heaven, and will say to the angels of glory: 'These are the gifts of little children. These are the gifts of poor men and hard-working women. These are the dollars and half dollars, the gifts of My children, and I wear them in memory of their love for Me.' "

So God will take your gifts and make crowns out of them and wear them for you and then hang them up as your memorial forevermore. But oh, I am so glad that He wears the crown first Himself. Yes, it is not you who is crowned—it is Jesus who is crowned. He wants you to bring your gifts, your sacrifices, your services, and give them to Him. He only is worthy. It was He who died for you. It was He who redeemed you. It was He who forgave you. It was He who took you back again. It was He who blessed you, lifted you, laid aside His crown for you. Now crown Him Lord of all.

Be like the dying woman who, when she could only say one word, gasped out the word "Bring." And they brought her water, and they brought her medicine, and they brought her her friends, and they brought her her children, and they brought her her husband, but she waved them all away. Mustering up her last strength, she said: "Bring forth the royal diadem, and crown Him Lord of all." And then, with her last breath, she just went up in a chariot of praise to His blessed arms.

CHAPTER 7

Finishing Our Work

I consider my life worth nothing to me, if only I may finish the race and complete the task the Lord Jesus has given me. (Acts 20:24)

This is a most serious thought, this thought of finishing our work. There is nothing, I think, in Christian life so sad as unfinished work.

There is no memorial in the cemetery that brings the tears to our eyes more quickly than the broken column which tells of a life broken in the midst. And as I look around me, I see so many broken columns in human life. Someone said to Napoleon, in one of his pageants in Africa under the shadow of the pyramids, as his veterans were marching in review: "Emperor, what is lacking here?" "Nothing, nothing," said he, "but continuance." He knew that in a little while these squadrons would dissolve and life itself would be perhaps a bitter disappointment. And so, in the work of God we have seen so much that was incomplete. I have seen so much in my own work that I have cried to God, that, even if He gave me a little work it would all be clear work—that it would be all finished work.

As I look over the work of God, I see this curse—uncompleted work—strewing the way all along with miserable wrecks. I find the book of Judges telling us of 500 years of declension because God's people did not complete their work when they were in possession of Canaan. They conquered Jericho. They conquered 31 kingdoms. They divided the land among 12 victorious tribes. But they left here and there little strongholds that were not subdued, little tribes that could not or would not be driven out. And it was not long until they brought Israel under subjection and neutralized all the work of Joshua's conquest.

I look again at the life of poor Saul, and I see that the one turning point in his life was where he stopped short of finishing God's work. He let his own fleshly heart control him, and because he left God's work unfinished, the curse of God's rejection fell upon him.

I look at the ministry of Elijah. The world has never seen anything more sublime than his victory on Mt. Carmel. But who has not wept at the reaction of the next day? At the shaking of a woman's finger he fled into the desert and left the field in possession of God's enemies. Israel never again recovered but went down and down, until it passed away, not in captivity, but in extinction.

Finishing Well

And so, it is not enough to go on for a while. It is the last step that wins. Oh, may God put on our hearts this great thought, "If only I may finish the race and complete the task the Lord Jesus has given me—the task of testifying to the gospel of God's grace" (Acts 20:24). How often this has been brought to my own heart, until it seemed to me that I could see nothing but just the closing days of life—the thought when it would all be finished and handed over to His hands. This verse provides two pictures. The one was the thought of much accomplished, but much lost; something done, but something undone; and the sad bitterness of the thought that it is almost better not to have lived than to have failed to complete my one life. The other picture was one of the soldier pressing on until the last hour, unflinching, unweary, afraid even of the thought of weariness. And, at last, looking back and saying, "By the grace of God there is nothing left out that the Lord had in His heart to give me to do. I have fought a good fight, I have finished my course. Henceforth it is all victory." And, as you go forth in this spirit, you will find that while you keep your eye on the end, it will give impulse and power to every step of the way.

The Work and Word of God

Then, as we look at finished work, how much of

it do we find in the work and Word of God.

We find, in the first chapter of Genesis, when God began the work of creation, He left nothing undone. So God finished, as we are told, the heavens and the earth, and God saw everything that He had made was good. Then He sat down and rested on His own Sabbath day. There was nothing left undone.

Take the most finished work of art and compare it with God's smallest creations. You will find the sting of the bee is superior to the most perfectly wrought needle that ever came from the factories or the tools of man. You find that the most perfect polished surface under the magnifying glass seems like a great mass of hills and valleys compared with the surface of your hand. The wing of the smallest insect is all spangled and shining with burnished, radiant splendor, and no matter how carefully you inspect it, there is no flaw—it is all perfect. You find the little blade of grass is made as carefully as the immense pine tree. All God's work is well done, and myriads of things seem to be made that produce no adequate return. On every side of us there are things that we do not seem to understand the use of. Everything is done with a prodigal bountifulness, and yet all are perfect.

We read about Moses that he finished his work. In the last chapter of Exodus, we have this description: "Moses did everything just as the LORD commanded him" (Exodus 40:16). His work was all done, and then God came in and took possession and made it His dwelling place. God does not want to come in and dwell in unfinished things. If you build a house and put no roof on it, it will fall to pieces, and so unfinished work will fail.

Again, we find that Joshua finished his work, and that was the secret of his power. "So Joshua took the entire land, just as the LORD had directed Moses" (Joshua 11:23). "He left nothing undone of all that the LORD commanded Moses" (11:15). He finished his work through and through, and all his life God's blessing was on that work and on the people. It was when Joshua passed away that they began slighting the work, and then came the declension and ruin of the period of the judges.

We read of Nehemiah that he finished his work. The prophet Zechariah had said about this restoration: "The hands of Zerubbabel have laid the foundation of this temple; his hands will also complete it. Then you will know that the LORD Almighty has sent me to you" (Zechariah 4:9). So we read about Nehemiah: "So the wall was completed on the twenty-fifth of Elul" (Nehemiah 6:15). There was no gate left out, no hinge broken, no break in the walls that was not completed, no unfinished work. Every little thing, every bar, every hinge, every rivet, was all secure. Then God blessed and established the work.

We read about the Lord Jesus that He finished His work. "I must be about my Father's business" (Luke 2:49, KJV). "As long as it is day, we must do the work of him who sent me. Night is coming" (John 9:4). " 'My food,' said Jesus, 'is to do the will of him who sent me and to finish his work' " (4:34). The hour came at last when He could say: "I have brought you glory on earth by completing the work you gave me to do. . . . I am coming to you now" (17:4, 13). His last word on the cross was "finished." When He arose from the grave there was such a wonderful quietness and deliberateness about Him, such an evidence of everything being orderly and completely done, that even the napkin was found wrapped together in a place by itself, and His grave clothes were all folded up in order. There was not a trifle left undone. The Lord did everything perfectly, easily and well.

We read about Paul that his one mission was to finish his course. The time came when, within the sight of the Ostian gate where he died, he could say: "I have fought the good fight, I have finished the race, I have kept the faith. Now there is in store for me the crown of righteousness, which the Lord, the righteous Judge, will award to me on that day—and not only to me, but also to all who have longed for his appearing" (2 Timothy 4:7-8). He finished his work, and, had he his life to live over again, perhaps there was nothing more he could have added to it.

Our Work

And now, dear friend, how about your work and mine? Let us look into it today. You are standing within a few steps of a borderline when this period of your life will close up forever. Have you accomplished that which you set out to do? Have you finished that which you began? How is it about your Christian character—is it entire, or is it incomplete? "May God himself, the God of peace, sanctify you through and through. May your whole spirit, soul and body be kept blameless at the coming of our Lord Jesus Christ" (1 Thessalonians 5:23).

Is that fulfilled, or are you only saved in spots, only cleansed here and there, with great blotches of sin upon you like a moth-eaten garment? That is not God's plan. God's idea for you is entire wholeness of character—your spirit, your soul, your body all sanctified unto Him. Why not? It is because you have not taken God's Word. It is because you have not been willing to enter into God's blessing and God's will. If you have not entered in here, it is not going to be any easier to enter into it anywhere else. Oh, before this day closes, just go to Him for that complete transformation. It is not a thing that you grow into. It is a thing that you take from Him as the free gift of His grace. May God help you today not to seek human perfection, but to take and have the perfect Christ reaching every part of your life, going ever in your complete being to mold you into a perfect child.

You know what it is to be a perfect babe. It is a poor, weak little thing, but it is perfect. You know what it is to have a poor, mutilated body with a hand off or an eye out. Now, God wants you to be a perfect child—to be complete, to be finished in all your parts, although with room for boundless expansion in the growth of your future life. The dear Savior has it for you, and you are slighting His costly purchase if you do not receive it.

Have you entered into the complete plan and purpose of God for your life? Paul prays for the Thessalonians that "God may count you worthy of his calling, and that by his power he may fulfill every good purpose of yours and every act prompted by your faith" (2 Thessalonians 1:11). Are you reaching out to that for which you were apprehended by Christ, or is God all the time having to drive you forward and press you on? God calls you to a complete conformity to His will that you may be holy and please God. He will give you the grace to do it.

How about your work; have you finished that? Have you started, and then got tired and dropped it? Have you been sent to some service, and at some little discouragement put it aside? Have you brought some soul to Christ and then left it again—never prayed for it, never sought to finish the trust that God gave to you? Have you promised anything and never fulfilled it? God calls us today to balance all our accounts with Him and to go away with the blessed thought that we have nothing more to do that could have been done. And He does not call us to anything unreasonable, extreme or impossible.

Even Samson, in the last moment of his life, accomplished a life's work in an hour. May God help you to accomplish the trust that has been committed to your hands, to leave nothing at last, undone.

Have you done what God has called you to do? Is it finished? Can we go to church with no raveled ends, with no loose, unfinished work? Can we go with that promptness and that obedience which God loves, and on which He pours out His perfect blessing, even in financial matters? He blesses His church for generosity quite as much as He does for faith and prayer and Christian work.

Is our life work going to be a completed scroll, or is it going to be a torn parchment, unfinished? I do not believe God wants it to be so for you or for me. Oh, what a precious life yours and mine is. Only once can it be lived. Never again can we traverse this ground. Remember as you go forth that you will never pass this way again. Let every earnest fiber of your being be laid at His feet, and do it as you would wish it done in that day when you will look back upon the life that will come no more. I say this for myself—I say it for you, dear friend. Someone has said:

> For at my back I always hear
> Time's swift-winged chariot hurrying near;
> And onward, all before, I see
> Deserts of vast eternity.

And Dr. Bonar reminds us:

> Not many lives have we—but one.
>   One, only one!

How precious should that one life be—
That narrow span!
Day after day filled up with faithful toil;
Year after year still bringing in new spoil.

I have heard somewhere of a poor fellow dying on the railroad track. As they picked him up all mangled, his face pale and blood flowing from every wound, he just had strength to say one sentence: "Oh, if only I had." Nobody knew that terrible regret that came surging up in his memory. Something he had meant to do and just put off that day. Something he had promised God to do but he did not, and never could it be done again. "Oh, if only I had." It speaks to me as the signal of an unfinished life—saved, perhaps, but not what God had saved it for. Coming in, but coming in to lose the crown God would have given. Happy, I hope. Oh yes, in heaven you will have happiness even in the lower place, but the one that could be content to take the lower place has got a mean soul and cannot be very happy anywhere.

It is said that one of the old translators of the Bible, as he was finishing his work, felt the cold damp of death coming over him. Calling his scribe, he said, "All is done but just one-half a chapter." And, as his pulses grew colder, he summoned up his faith and courage, and called to his secretary, and said; "Write quickly." He began to dictate, and words poured from his lips as fast as the hand could write. "Be quick," he said, "be quick, the sands are running out." The words